AQA Music

Andrew S Coxon
Robert Chapman

Nelson Thornes

Published in 2009 by:
Nelson Thornes Ltd
Delta Place
27 Bath Road
CHELTENHAM
GL53 7TH
United Kingdom

09 10 11 12 13 / 10 9 8 7 6 5 4 3 2 1

A catalogue record for this book is available from the British Library

ISBN 978 1 4085 0420 8

Illustrations by David Russell Illustration

Page make-up by Hart McLeod, Cambridge

Printed and bound in Spain by GraphyCems

Acknowledgements

The authors and publisher are grateful to the following for permission to reproduce copyright material:

Photographs:

Cover photograph: courtesy of Photolibrary/Stockbyte

iv Getty Images; Chapter 1 banner Alamy/The Photolibrary Wales; 1.2A Corbis/Chuck Savage; Chapter 2 banner Corbis/Penny Tweedie; 2.3A Lebrecht; 2.9A Arenapal; 2.9B Corbis/Penny Tweedie; 2.10A Mike Booth/Alamy; 2.12C and 2.14B Lebrecht; Chapter 3 banner Corbis/Sandro Vannini; 3.1A Lebrecht Music & Arts Photo Library;3.1B The London Art Archive/Alamy; 3.5A Redferns/Ron Scherl; 3.6A Alamy; 3.7A Arenapal; Chapter 4 banner and 4.0 Getty/Redferns/David Redfern; 4.1 (right) Arenapal/Topfoto; 4.2A SNAP/Rex Features; 4.2 (right) Redferns/ David Redfern; 4.3A Scott Hortop Travel/Alamy; 4.3B Redferns/Val Wilmer; 4.4A Redferns/GAB Archives; 4.5A iStockphoto.com; 4.6A Rex/Alastair Muir; 4.8A Lebrecht Music & Arts Photo Library; Chapter 5 banner Alamy/Peter Titmuss; 5.1 (left) Alamy/Peter Titmuss; 5.2A Getty/Redferns; 5.3A Alamy/GFC Collection; 5.3B Alamy/Randy Duchaine; 5.3C www.drumbum.com; 5.3D Alamy/Philip Scalia; 5.4A Alamy/Dave Thompson; 5.4B Alamy/Neil McAllister; 5.4C Lebrecht; 5.4D Lebrecht; 5.4E Lebrecht/Dinodia Images; 5.5B Alamy/Devinder Sangha; Chapter 6 banner and 6.0 Corbis/Phil Schermeister; 6.1A Alan Shaw/Alamy; 6.2C iStockphoto; Chapter 7 banner and 7.0 Alamy/Jupiter Images; 7.3B/C/D Lebrecht; 7.4A/B Lebrecht; 7.4C DK Images; 7.5B Everett Collection/Rex Features; 7.6A Redferns/Anthony Pidgeon; 7.7A Arenapal; 7.8A Arenapal; 7.8B www.Steinberg.net; 7.9A Corbis; 7.10D Lucidio Studio Inc./Corbis; 7.12C Julian Winslow/Corbis; 7.13A Peter Nickol; 7.15C Ant Strack/Corbis; 7.15E Lebrecht; Chapter 8 banner and 8.0 Alamy/Ian Shaw; 8.3A Fancy/Veer/Corbis; 8.3B Richard T. Nowitz/CORBIS; Chapter 9 banner and 9.0 Alamy/Pixonnet.com; 9.1 (left) Tom Merton/Getty; 9.3 (right) Tetra Images/Alamy; Chapter banner and 10.0 Alamy/Ian Shaw; 10.2B AQA; Chapter 11 banner and 11.0 Alamy/ Lebrecht; 11.1A Alamy/J.R. Bale; 11.1B Corbis; 11.2A Redferns/Andrew Lepley; 11.2B bilderlounge/Alamy; Chapter 12 banner and 12.0 Alamy/J.R. Bale; 12.1A/B Jazz Badgers; 12.3A ArenaPAL/Elliott Franks; Chapter 13 banner and 13.0 Alamy/Ian Shaw; 13.1B Tim Pannell/Corbis; 13.1C Will & Deni McIntyre/CORBIS; 13.2A Lebrecht

Audio CD edited and mastered by www.ffg.org.uk

Contents

Introduction 5
Foreword 6

1 The new GCSE course 7
1.1 About the examination 8
1.2 What the book contains 10

UNIT ONE Listening and Appraising

2 The five Areas of Study and the three Strands of Learning 13
2.1 Rhythm and metre 14
2.2 Rhythm and metre 16
2.3 Harmony and tonality 18
2.4 Harmony and tonality 20
2.5 Harmony and tonality 22
2.6 Texture and melody 24
2.7 Texture and melody 26
2.8 Texture and melody 28
2.9 Timbre and dynamics 30
2.10 Timbre and dynamics 32
2.11 Timbre and dynamics 34
2.12 Structure and form 36
2.13 Structure and form 38
2.14 Structure and form 40
2.15 The three Strands of Learning 42

3 The Western Classical tradition 45
3.1 The baroque orchestra 46
3.2 Baroque genres 48
3.3 The concerto 50
3.4 Music for voices: choral music 52
3.5 Music for voices: operas and songs 54
3.6 Chamber music 56
3.7 The sonata 58

4 Popular music of the 20th and 21st centuries 61
4.1 The blues 62
4.2 Popular music of the 1960s: the beginnings 64
4.3 Popular music of the 1960s: other forms 66
4.4 British popular music in the 1960s 68
4.5 Rock music 70
4.6 Hip-hop and music theatre 72
4.8 Film music 74

5 World music 77
5.1 Music of the Caribbean 78
5.2 Music of Africa: choral and popular music 80
5.3 Music of Africa: drumming and instrumental music 82
5.4 Music of India: background and instruments 84
5.5 Music of India: classical and popular styles 86

UNITS TWO AND FOUR Composing

6 Introduction to composition 89
6.1 What you have to do 90
6.2 Approaching composition 92

7 Developing composing skills 95
7.1 Musical elements: rhythm and metre (AoS1) 96

7.2	Musical elements: harmony and tonality (AoS2)	98
7.3	Musical elements: texture and melody (AoS3)	100
7.4	Musical elements: timbre and dynamics (AoS4)	102
7.5	Musical elements: structure and form (AoS5)	104
7.6	The elements combined	106
7.7	Instrumental and vocal combinations	108
7.8	ICT	110
7.9	What should I bear in mind?	112
7.10	Writing it down	114
7.11	Writing it down: staff notation and graphic notation	116
7.12	Writing it down: tab and written account (annotation)	118
7.13	Writing it down: what is right for me?	120
7.14	Listening and study: introduction	122
7.15	Combinations of the musical elements	124
7.16	Further study	126

8 **Choosing the area of composition** **129**

8.1	Informing choice	130
8.2	Starting to write	132
8.3	Writing more	134

9 **Appraising your composition** **137**

9.1	The appraisal	138
9.2	How to prepare and plan	140
9.3	Further practice	142

10 **Managing your time** **145**

10.1	Preparing for the examination	146
10.2	Final recording and presentation	148

UNIT THREE Performing

11 **Making choices** **151**

11.1	About this component	152
11.2	Choosing an option	154

12 **Developing skills** **157**

12.1	Acoustic performances: solo and group	158
12.2	What are they looking for?	160
12.3	Acoustic performance: rapping and turntablism	162
12.4	Technology-based performances	164
12.5	What are they looking for?	166

13 **Preparing your performance** **169**

13.1	Acoustic performance	170
13.2	Technology-based performances	172
13.3	Presenting an annotation	174

CD track listing	177
Quiz answers	180
Glossary	183
Index	189

Nelson Thornes has worked in partnership with AQA to ensure this book and the accompanying online resources offer you the best support for your GCSE course.

All resources have been approved by senior AQA examiners so you can feel assured that they closely match the specification for this subject and provide you with everything you need to prepare successfully for your exams.

These print and online resources together **unlock blended learning**; this means that the links between the activities in the book and the activities online blend together to maximise your understanding of a topic and help you achieve your potential.

These online resources are available on which can be accessed via the internet at **http://www.kerboodle.com/live**, anytime, anywhere. If your school or college subscribes to kerboodle! you will be provided with your own personal login details. Once logged in, access your course and locate the required activity.

For more information and help on how to use kerboodle! visit **http://www.kerboodle.com**.

How to use this book

Objectives

Look for the list of **Learning Objectives** based on the requirements of this course so you can ensure you are covering everything you need to know for the exam.

AQA Examiner's tip

Don't forget to read the **AQA Examiner's Tips** throughout the book.

Visit **http://www.nelsonthornes.com/aqagcse** for more information.

The Controlled Assessment tasks in this book are designed to help you prepare for the tasks your teacher will give you. The tasks in this book are not designed to test you formally and you cannot use them as your own Controlled Assessment tasks for AQA. Your teacher will not be able to give you as much help with your tasks for AQA as we have given with the tasks in this book.

Foreword

Once, a few years ago, when I was working with a group of music teachers, I remember saying that even though teaching GCSE music can be hard, actually doing the course as a KS4 student is harder! Anything that can directly help students perform better in their coursework by improving their understanding should therefore be valued by student and teacher alike.

This book has been written by experienced teachers, examiners and moderators, primarily to help students preparing for the AQA examination in GCSE Music. It is intended to help and complement the work of classroom teachers, not to replace that work. It should help individual students to assess their knowledge, identify areas on which to concentrate their study, and master key concepts to help them succeed in GCSE coursework, thus improving their final outcomes in the exam.

The book is filled with information and ideas that will help students master the skills needed to do well in the various elements of the examination. It aims to help students concentrate on what is important in the different areas of the course, to maximise their potential, and to cope effectively with the requirements of the AQA GCSE Music Specification.

While acknowledging the fact that not everyone responds in the same way to the same delivery, a blended learning solution that combines teacher-led learning and self-study will help all students enormously.

The book is divided into chapters based on:

- listening and appraising
- composition
- performance.

Enjoy – and good luck in the exam!

Phil Redding

AQA GCSE Music Coursework Adviser and Team Leader

November 2008

Objectives

In this chapter you will learn:

about the content of the new GCSE course and how it will be covered by this book

about the various units within the course

an outline of the specification

how to use this book.

Introduction

The aim of this book is to guide you through the new AQA GCSE course. There is no single way of approaching your studies, but you must remember that the whole course is based on the elements of music that form the five **Areas of Study** (AoS). You will approach these through three **Strands of Learning**. The Areas of Study and Strands of Learning are listed at the start of Chapter 2.

Each of the four units is based directly on the Areas of Study. At the end of the course, you will be assessed through:

- a listening and appraising examination (Unit 1)
- a composition and its appraisal (Unit 2)
- two performances (which include the option of using technology) (Unit 3)
- a further composition (Unit 4).

This book will help you gain the skills you need to succeed in AQA's GCSE Music specification. There is guidance on each of the four units, but the order in which you approach them can be flexible. Students will come to this book with differing levels of skill and experience, so you may need to study some areas in greater detail than others. However, whatever your starting level, you need to prepare and help yourself in this course by listening to a wide range of music from different periods, styles and genres; you should perform music both individually and as part of a group; you should work with music technology; and you should compose music for different purposes and media.

Each section starts with a list of Learning Objectives, and each chapter ends with both a Summary and a Revision Quiz.

Other features include:

- Key terms: an explanation of musical terms to help your understanding
- Examiner's tips: helpful advice from an AQA examiner/ moderator
- Activities: structured activities to help you practise the skills covered, or prepare for the examination
- Did you know? Interesting background to ideas covered in the main text
- Remember: key points to be borne in mind
- ♫ Listening activities

The specification structure

The GCSE specification consists of four units:

Unit 1: Listening to and Appraising Music

Unit 2: Composing and Appraising Music

Unit 3: Performing Music

Unit 4: Composing Music

Units 1 and 2 will be assessed by an examination at the end of the course. Units 3 and 4 will be assessed initially by the teacher and then sent to an AQA-appointed moderator.

Assessment Objectives

The three Assessment Objectives are common to all music courses:

AO1 Performing skills: performing/realising with technical control, expression and interpretation

AO2 Composing skills: creating and developing musical ideas with technical control and coherence

AO3 Listening and appraising skills: analysing and evaluating music using musical terminology

Objectives
You will learn:
about the new AQA GCSE Music specification
about the content of the four units
about the three assessment objectives
about the weighting of the different assessment objectives.

A *Assessment Objectives and unit weightings allocation within the specification*

Assessment Objectives	Unit weightings (%)				Overall weighting of AOs (%)
	1	2	Controlled Assessment		
			3	4	
AO1 Performing skills			40		40
AO2 Composing skills		10		20	30
AO3 Listening/Appraising skills	20	10			30
Overall weighting of units (%)	20	20	40	20	100

The four units

Unit 1: Listening to and Appraising Music

This makes up 20 per cent of the final mark, and is assessed by an examination of one hour with questions on short excerpts of music. The questions will be based on the musical terms listed in the specification; you will not be asked about anything outside this list. The examination is marked by AQA examiners.

Unit 2: Composing and Appraising Music

This makes up 20 per cent of the final marks, divided between a composition (10 per cent) and an appraisal (10 per cent). The composition will explore at least two of the Areas of Study and will link to the strand chosen by the examination board – this will change each year. You will have up to 20 hours of supervised time in which to complete this composition. Your appraisal will be written in an appraisal booklet, which will contain questions to help you structure your response. This will be done during a further two hours of controlled time. This examination is marked by AQA examiners.

Unit 3: Performing Music

This makes up 40 per cent of the final marks. Your teacher will mark the performances, and then they will be assessed again by an AQA moderator. You will perform a solo piece (acoustic or technology-based) and a group performance. These performances can be recorded at any point during the course. Performances are to be recorded in a format that can be played on an external device such as CD or minidisc. MP3 files *must not* be sent to the moderator.

Unit 4: Composing Music

This makes up 20 per cent of the final marks. Your teacher will mark the composition, and then it will be assessed again by an AQA moderator. You will compose one piece of music exploring at least two of the Areas of Study: the music can be in any style or genre of your choosing. You will have up to 25 hours of controlled time in which to complete the composition.

All compositions must be recorded in a format that can be played on an external device such as CD or minidisc. Recordings of compositions may be made using live performers, ICT or a combination of both. MP3 files *must not* be sent to the moderator.

All compositions and performances must be accompanied by a musical score: a score is understood to be any written format that is appropriate to the particular genre of music presented. However, for the *compositions* it must make clear exactly what the composer intended, and for the *performances* it must enable the teacher and moderator to understand exactly what the candidate's role in the performance is.

Candidate Record Form

For each of Units 2, 3 and 4 you will also have to submit a Candidate Record Form (CRF). Advice and guidance on how to complete these will be given with each individual unit.

This student handbook explains what you will have to do for each of the four units, and how each unit will be assessed. Advice is offered on how to do well and prepare thoroughly to meet the requirements of each unit. The amount of time you will need to spend on each section will depend on your abilities and experience.

Objectives

You will learn:

what is included in the book

how to use the information.

Unit 1: Listening to and Appraising Music

The elements of music that form the five Areas of Study are approached through three Strands of Learning. The book explores these in detail, introducing you to the different styles and genres listed in the specification. It will guide you through the music related to the three strands, using particular pieces of music as case studies for closer examination and analysis, with excerpts recorded on a CD which is also available. How composers have combined the elements within their music is discussed and explained.

Certain popular tracks discussed in the book were not possible to include on the CD, but these are well known and widely available both on CD and as downloads, and it is hoped that they will be easy to obtain. See page 177 for details of the tracks referred to in this book and some suggested listening.

Attention is paid to the types of question which may arise in the final examination. Your teacher can obtain a specimen test from the examination board (comprising a CD, question paper plus answer booklet, and mark scheme). All questions in the final examination paper will be based on excerpts of music and will test your listening skills.

Unit 2: Composing and Appraising Music

In this unit, 10 per cent is awarded for your composition and 10 per cent for your appraisal. Initially, this section will focus on the five Areas of Study and investigate ways in which they can be used as the basis for composing. From there, the AoS are featured in pairs, with suggestions for styles/genres of compositions and ways in which they can be linked to one of the three strands.

Ways of starting compositions will be discussed and practical examples given. These openings will then be extended with advice on how this can be applied to your own work. There are examples of compositions on the available CD. At the heart of composing is the use of a composer's notebook for recording all your musical ideas, even those which don't turn out well. Guidance on the production of a musical score is also given.

The section on appraising your composition will start from the questions given for your guidance in the appraisal booklet, and will offer advice and guidance on how to respond successfully.

Guidance is given on how to prepare for and make best use of the controlled time allowed for composing and appraising.

■ Unit 3: Performing Music

In this unit, 20 per cent is awarded to each of two performances, one individual (acoustic or technology-based), the other a group performance. This section explains what you will need to do for this unit, and offers advice on which solo option to choose. We will give you guidance on how to make sure your performances are successful, and practical advice on how to choose your repertoire and prepare for your final performance and submission.

The way your performance will be assessed is explained fully.

■ Unit 4: Composing Music

You will compose a second piece of music combining at least two of the Areas of Study. You can write in any style or genre you choose. The guidance is essentially the same as that outlined for Unit 2, but for this unit you can choose from a wider choice of styles or genres, so you might decide to be creative in a different style (although you don't have to).

A *Composing music*

1

In this chapter you have learnt:

- ✔ about the content of the GCSE course
- ✔ about the content of each of the four units
- ✔ about the three Assessment Objectives
- ✔ about the percentage weighting of each of the units
- ✔ about the method of examination for each unit
- ✔ how this handbook is organised
- ✔ how to use this handbook.

Revision quiz

1. What are the four units that make up this specification?
2. What are the three Assessment Objectives?
3. Give a brief explanation of what each actually assesses.
4. Which of the four units carries the highest percentage of marks?
5. Unit 2 has two sections: what are they?
6. In Unit 2, is either of the two sections worth more than the other?
7. In Unit 3, what are the two options for the individual performance?
8. For this specification, what is meant by a musical score?
9. How many Areas of Study are there?
10. How many Strands of Learning are there?
11. Which of the composing units must have a link to a Strand of Learning?
12. Which units are assessed by your teacher first?

2 The five Areas of Study and three Strands of Learning

Objectives

In this chapter you will learn:

about the five Areas of Study

about the three Strands of Learning

about the relationship between the Areas of Study and the Strands of Learning

about how they link to the composition coursework.

▓ Introduction

This chapter explores the five Areas of Study (AoS), which are central to all of the units. They cover the main elements of music, grouped in pairs as follows:

AoS 1: rhythm and metre

AoS 2: harmony and tonality

AoS 3: texture and melody

AoS 4: timbre and dynamics

AoS 5: structure and form

You will also learn about the three Strands of Learning:

- The Western Classical tradition
- Popular music of the 20th and 21st centuries
- World music.

Each strand contains different styles or genres which may be used in the excerpts, but you will not be tested on your knowledge of these in the listening test: questions will focus on aspects of the five Areas of Study. You will also have to link your composing coursework in Unit 2 to one of the three strands.

Starter activity

Listen to different pieces of music from recordings or from performances by your friends or school ensembles. Make a list of the features you can already recognise from the five Areas of Study.

2.1　Rhythm and metre

This is all about beats, timing and sound patterns. A **metre** is a regular pattern of **beats** indicated by a **time signature**. A **rhythm** is the way different lengths of sound are combined to produce patterns in time.

You will need to learn the following terms and be able to recognise them, or comment on their use in short musical extracts:

- pulse
- simple and compound time
- regular, irregular and free rhythms
- augmentation, diminution, hemiola, cross-rhythm
- dotted rhythms, triplets, syncopation
- tempo, rubato
- polyrhythm, bi-rhythm
- drum fills.

Pulse and time signatures

The pulse is the beat of the music. It is what you tap your feet to. Although the music may have rhythms made up of different lengths of notes, the pulse or beat will be steady.

There are two types of time signature: simple and compound time. In simple time each beat is divided into two equal parts. Examples of simple time signatures are:

2/4　3/4　4/4

(Within text, these are commonly written like fractions – 2/4, 3/4, 4/4 – even though they are not actually fractions.)

In compound time each beat is divided into three equal parts. Examples of compound time signatures are 6/8, 9/8, 12/8. A feature of compound time signatures is their use of **dotted notes**.

Regular and irregular rhythms

Most western music has regular rhythms. This means that when you listen to a piece of music you can feel (perhaps by tapping your fingers or a foot) that it is made up of regular groups (**bars**) of pulses (**beats**). This is the 'time' or 'metre' of the music. Regular rhythms occur in duple time (2 beats to a bar, e.g. 2/4, 6/8), triple time (3 beats to a bar, e.g. 3/4, 9/8) or quadruple time (4 beats to a bar, e.g. 4/4, 12/8). The important thing is to hear when the first beat of a new bar occurs, as this will help you to work out the metre and time signature. The first beat carries the strongest accent. This does not necessarily mean that it will have a louder note, but you should try to 'feel' the beat by tapping or counting rhythmically.

Irregular rhythms are those that do not fit into the usual rhythmic patterns of duple, triple or quadruple times mentioned above. Irregular rhythms often have time signatures such as 5/4, 5/8, 7/4, 7/8, where each bar is made up of combinations of two- and three-beat note patterns. Compare the 4/4 and 6/8 rhythmic patterns below with 5/4 and 5/8. Note where the strong and secondary accents (printed in bold) occur, and how the beats form regular groups in 4/4 and 6/8 but irregular groups in 5/4 and 5/8.

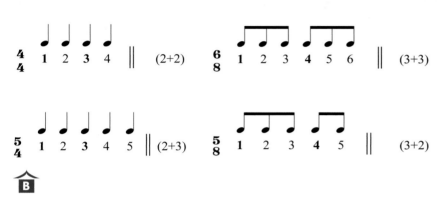

> **AQA *Examiner's tip***
>
> If you are asked to identify a particular kind of rhythm or time signature, try to 'feel' the pulse or beat. Work out if it is duple, triple or quadruple first, and whether it is simple or compound time, as described earlier. If it does not appear to fit any of those, try irregular time signatures. Don't worry if you can't decide whether a piece is in duple or quadruple time, e.g. 2/4 or 4/4. You will not be penalised in the examination because duple and quadruple metres are so similar.

Free rhythms

Music that is in free rhythm has no definite metre or pulse. In this kind of music you will not be able to detect a regular or irregular pattern of beats. Accents may come in different places, giving the impression that the time signature changes every bar, or you may feel that there is no real accent or pulse.

2.2　Rhythm and metre

Augmentation, diminution, hemiola, cross-rhythm and syncopation

Objectives

You will learn:

about the other elements that make up rhythm and metre.

These are all examples of rhythmic devices.

Augmentation is where a melody or series of notes is repeated using notes of a longer duration. For example, a melody with an original rhythm of:

might be played:

Diminution is the opposite: the note-lengths of the original melody are shortened when it is played again.

A **hemiola** rhythm has a 'three against two' metrical feel. For example, in this 3/4 rhythm there is a hemiola in the last two bars, giving the impression of three minim beats in two bars of 3/4 time.

Hemiolas are found in all types of music, but were often used in dance music during the **Renaissance** and **Baroque** periods, where they give the regular 3/4 pulse a rhythmic 'kick'.

A **cross-rhythm** occurs when two different rhythms are played together at the same time. Usually the rhythms contrast in some way, for instance a rhythm with a triple metre feel against a rhythm with a duple or quadruple metre feel.

Syncopation occurs when a composer changes the usual stress of the beats in a bar. This might be by placing an accent on a weak beat or part of a beat, or by placing a rest on a strong beat, for example:

It is a common rhythmic feature of many musical styles, particularly popular music and dance music.

Key terms

Renaissance: music typically composed between about 1450 and 1600.

Baroque: style of music composed between about 1600 and 1750.

Tempo and rubato

Tempo is the speed of the music, the speed at which you count the beats. This is often indicated either by an Italian word or by a metronome marking, or both, and will not change in a piece of music unless indicated.

However, performers sometimes speed up or slow down, even if not indicated, in response to the way the music makes them feel. These unwritten tempo changes are called **rubato**. Sometimes composers add the words *rubato* or *tempo rubato* to the score, indicating that they do not want a strict tempo.

Polyrhythm, bi-rhythm and drum fills

A **polyrhythmic** texture is created when two or more different rhythms are played at the same time. Like cross-rhythms, the parts usually contrast in metre and accent, producing a rich, complex texture. They are often found in African and Afro-Cuban music. A **bi-rhythm** is a specific type of polyrhythm, consisting of two independent rhythms played simultaneously.

A 'fill' is a short passage of music which helps to bridge the gaps between sections or phrases of a melody in a piece of music. Any instrument can do this, but the **drum fill** has become a regular feature of much popular music. Most pop styles have their own characteristic fills, but in general they are all short and simple and do not change the tempo, so that the flow of the music is maintained.

> **AQA** *Examiner's tip*
>
> Find out the tempo directions of pieces you play or listen to, and get a feeling for the beat and tempo. Use a metronome and become familiar with the Italian terms and how they relate to the tempo. Metronome markings are measured in beats per minute (bpm).

2.3 Harmony and tonality

▇ What is harmony?

Harmony occurs when two notes of different pitch are sounded together. However, it's a bit more complicated than that! When we think of harmony we usually mean the notes that accompany a melody. Harmony has the power to make a melody richer and more emotional.

▇ What will you need to learn?

There are many different types of harmony and harmonic devices. You will need to learn the following terms and be able to recognise them, or comment on their use in short musical extracts:

- diatonic, chromatic
- consonant, dissonant
- pedal, drone
- cadence: perfect, plagal, imperfect, interrupted, *tierce de Picardie*
- major, minor and dominant seventh chords using Roman numerals or chord symbols.

Diatonic, chromatic

Diatonic harmony uses only notes that belong to the **scale** or **key** that the music is written in. For example, if a piece of music is in the key of C major, it will mainly use the notes of the C major scale:

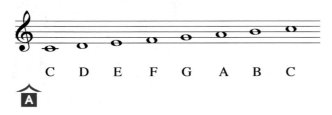

C   D   E   F   G   A   B   C

A

Diatonic harmony will only use notes from the same scale. **Chromatic** harmony uses other notes as well. For example, in the key of C major any sharps ♯ or flats ♭ (the black notes on a keyboard) which are used in the harmony do not belong to the scale or key of C major. They are **chromatic** notes. Chromatic means 'colour', and these notes are used to add colour to the harmony, helping to enhance the emotional effect of the music.

Consonant, dissonant

When you listen to a piece of music you might think the harmony is pleasant and nice. Or you might think it clashes and sounds uncomfortable, even painful to listen to. The first, pleasant kind of harmony is **consonant**. This kind of harmony sounds agreeable. **Dissonant** harmony, on the other hand, really clashes. It is often used to create suspense or tension in a composition, and feels as if it needs to move towards more pleasing consonant harmonies to sound finished.

Listening activity

Listen to or play examples of music that use diatonic or chromatic harmony, so that you can hear the difference. Discuss the effect they create. Try playing diatonic chords on a keyboard, perhaps to one of your own compositions, and then altering one or more of the notes to make a chromatic chord. What difference does it make to the mood of the piece?

Pedal, drone

A **pedal note** is sustained (held) or repeated, while the harmonies change. It can be 'doubled', adding the same note an octave higher or lower. You need to listen carefully to the harmony, because this must change to at least one other chord. If the harmony does not change, it is not a pedal note. Pedal notes are usually in the bass, but sometimes they are higher than the melody; this is called an **inverted pedal**.

A drone is played in the bass. It can be just one note, like a pedal, but often has two notes played at the same time (for example, the drone played on bagpipes). These two notes are usually a fifth apart, for example C and G, played in the bass, below the melody. They may be sustained or repeated. Drones are often used to accompany melodies in **folk music** or **medieval music**, particularly dance music.

Key terms

Folk music: composed by ordinary people. It was not originally written down, but passed on from one person to another. The harmony is often played on instruments that can play a drone, such as bagpipes.

Medieval music: composed between about 400 and 1450.

A *Folk musicians*

2.4   Harmony and tonality

Degrees of the scale

Notes can be identified by letter names (A B C etc.), but when they form a scale they can be identified by Roman numerals (I II III etc.) or by special names which indicate the degree of the scale: tonic, supertonic, mediant, etc. For instance, here are the notes of the C major scale:

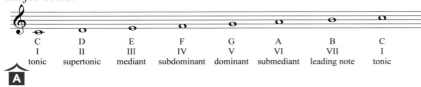

Cadences

A cadence is formed by the two chords that come at the end of a musical phrase. Cadences are a kind of 'musical punctuation', like full stops or commas. There are four main kinds of cadence:

Perfect cadence

This is made up of two chords: the dominant (chord V), which is the chord built on the fifth note of the scale, followed by the tonic (chord I), built on the first note of the scale. A perfect cadence is like a full stop. It gives the music a sense of completion.

Plagal cadence

This has the subdominant chord (chord IV) followed by the tonic (chord I). It is another example of a 'full stop', but is not as strong as a perfect cadence. It is sometimes called an 'amen' cadence, because it is often used to harmonise this word at the end of hymns.

Imperfect cadence

This has the opposite effect. It acts as a musical comma: the music must move on after it. An imperfect cadence is made up of any chord – but typically chord I, II or IV – followed by the dominant chord (V).

Interrupted cadence

This is sometimes called a 'surprise cadence'. It is quite easy to recognise. It starts with chord V, but, instead of being followed by the expected tonic chord (I), it goes to the submediant chord (VI). Chord VI is a chord of opposites: in a major key it is a minor chord, in a minor key it is a major chord – there's the surprise! It is another example of a musical comma; the music must move on to finish.

Did you know ?????

A *tierce de Picardie* is a very special kind of cadence. This is when the final chord of a piece or movement in a minor key is a tonic major chord instead of the expected tonic minor chord. For example, if a piece or movement is in C minor, the last chord, unexpectedly, would be C major.

Activity

1   Play or listen to pieces that have examples of all of the different cadences shown on this page, so that you can recognise them by listening.

B Cadences in C major

Perfect cadence   Plagal cadence   Imperfect cadence   Interrupted cadence

Chords – major and minor

A **chord** has two or more notes of different pitch sounded together. The most common type of chord has three different notes. It is called a **triad**. Triads can be built on any note in a scale. The lowest note is the one that gives the chord its name; it is called the 'root'. Above it we add notes a 3rd and a 5th above the root. It is important to count the root as number 1 when working out the notes above it.

Chords can be named by the letter name of their root, or from their position in a scale by using Roman numerals:

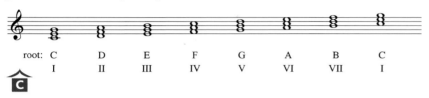

root:	C	D	E	F	G	A	B	C
	I	II	III	IV	V	VI	VII	I

This is useful in identifying chords when we change to a different scale or key.

> ### Activity
>
> **2** Play the triads (chords) built on the notes in the scale of C major on an instrument which can play chords, such as a keyboard or guitar. Listen to the major chords (I, IV and V, or chords C, F and G) and compare them to the minor chords (II, III and VI, or Dm, Em and Am). Try changing a major chord to a minor chord by playing the middle note (the 3rd) a semitone lower, or changing a minor chord to a major chord by playing the middle note a semitone higher.

We can build up a fuller-sounding chord by adding a fourth note to a triad. One way is to 'double' a note that already exists in the triad, an octave higher or lower. For example:

Dominant seventh chords

However, a special four-note chord can be built on the dominant – chord V. Instead of doubling one of the triad notes we add a new note seven notes above the root.

In C major, for example, chord V is:

Adding the 7th above the root, we get:

This is an example of a seventh chord, because it is made up of notes a 3rd, a 5th and a 7th above the root. A seventh chord built on the dominant is called a **dominant seventh** (V7), and is an alternative to chord V.

Key terms

Chord: two or more notes of different pitch played together.

Triad: the most common type of chord, made up of three notes. The lowest note, which gives the chord its letter name, is called the 'root'. The notes above it are a 3rd and a 5th above the root.

Remember

Triads can be major or minor. The difference is that the middle note (the 3rd) is a semitone lower in a minor chord than a major. In a major scale, the major chords are I, IV and V. The others are minor chords, except chord VII. This is an example of a diminished chord, which you will not need to recognise for GCSE.

AQA Examiner's tip

In the examination you will be tested on recognising harmony aurally – by listening. Try to listen to and play different kinds of music that can help you recognise the harmonic features you have studied.

2.5　Harmony and tonality

What is meant by 'tonality'?

Tonality means that the music belongs to a key: it is built mainly from the notes of a particular scale. The strongest note in any scale is the **tonic** (the note the scale starts and ends on). This has an effect on the other notes in the scale; in tonal music there is always the feeling that the music needs to end on the tonic. This also applies to the harmony, since chords are built on notes of the scale. Chord I is the **tonic chord**.

What will you need to learn?

- major, minor and modal tonalities
- identification of keys up to 4 sharps and 4 flats
- modulation to the dominant in major or minor keys, or to the relative major or minor.

Major and minor scales

We have already looked at scales and keys. Scales are made up of tones and semitones. In a major scale the semitones always occur between the 3rd and 4th, and the 7th and 8th notes of the scale.

Activity

1　Play the notes of the C major scale on a keyboard. Notice that there are black notes between all the white notes except E and F, and B and C, which are a semitone apart.

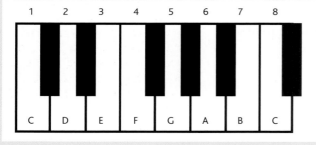

In a minor scale, the most important difference is that the 3rd note is lowered by a semitone.

Activity

2　Play the first five notes of the C minor scale on a keyboard. Compare it with C major. Listen to the difference between the E ♮ in C major, and the E ♭ in C minor.

Activity

3　Listen to or play pieces in major and minor keys. How does being in a major or minor key affect the music?

Key signatures in major and minor keys

Because a major scale must have semitones between the 3rd and 4th, and 7th and 8th notes of the scale, C major is the only major scale which can be played only using the white notes of a keyboard. If we start a major scale on any other note we will have to use the black notes – sharps ♯ and flats ♭ – to make the semitones occur in the right place. In notation, instead of writing the sharps or flats each time they occur, they are written at the beginning of each stave, after the clef. This is called a **key signature**.

Minor keys also have different key signatures, depending on their starting note. For each major key there is a minor key that shares the same key signature. In this case the minor key is called the **relative minor**. Relative minors are always a 3rd lower than their relative major key. In a minor scale the 7th note (leading note) is often raised by a semitone, but this is not part of the key signature.

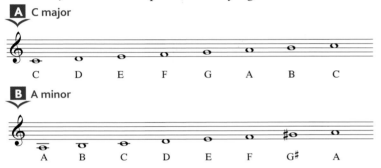

You will need to learn the key signatures up to four sharps and flats.

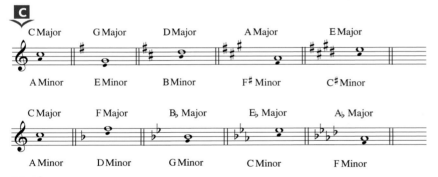

Modes

Modes are ancient scales, and are very distinctive. Each mode has a different structure of tones and semitones, unlike major and minor scales – though they sometimes sound like a mixture of the two. Unlike major and minor scales, where there is a semitone between the 7th (leading note) and 8th (tonic) notes of the scale, most modes have a tone between the 7th and 8th notes. This gives the music a distinctive character which you should listen for. In ancient Greece, the modes were identified and given names.

Modulation

Modulation is when the music changes key. In the examination you may have to recognise modulations from the tonic key. These will be either to the dominant (the key a 5th above the tonic) or to the relative major or minor.

2.6   Texture and melody

What is meant by 'texture'

Texture describes how much is going on in the music at any one time. It is about the different ways instruments and voices are combined in a piece of music.

You will need to be able to recognise the following textures:

- harmonic/homophonic, polyphonic/contrapuntal
- broken chords
- imitative, canonic, layered
- unison, octaves, single melody line, melody with accompaniment, antiphonal.

Harmonic/homophonic

These terms, referring to texture, mean the same thing: a texture that is essentially **chordal**. It may also be described as a **melody** with **accompaniment**, since the melody line is the most important. The melody is usually, but not always, at the top of the texture, with other parts providing some kind of chordal accompaniment.

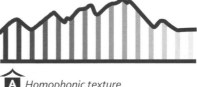

A *Homophonic texture*

Activity

1   Play or listen to all the different parts in a hymn tune. The melody is usually the top (highest) part of the texture. The other parts support the melody by providing a harmonic accompaniment made up of chords. This is a typical harmonic/homophonic texture.

Broken chords

It is possible to play the notes of a chord separately, one after the other. This is called a **broken chord**. Broken chord patterns provide a more gentle, flowing accompaniment to a melody than when the chord notes are played together.

Activity

2   A popular type of broken chord pattern is the 'Alberti bass'. Find an example of a piece of music which uses an Alberti bass, play or listen to it, and compare it with the chords used in hymn tunes, where the chord notes are played (or sung) together.

Polyphonic/contrapuntal

These terms also mean the same thing, but are very different from a harmonic/homophonic texture. A **polyphonic/contrapuntal** texture consists of weaving together two or more equally important melodic lines, which all fit together harmonically. A polyphonic/contrapuntal texture typically sounds 'busy'.

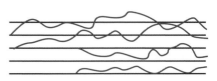

B *Polyphonic texture*

Imitative, canonic

To **imitate** means to copy, and this is exactly what happens in the music. One vocal or instrumental part starts off playing a melody, which is immediately copied, or imitated, by another voice or instrumental part, though not necesarily at the same pitch. Usually, it is only the first few notes of the melody which are imitated, and several voices or instrumental parts may take turns to imitate the opening of the original melody.

A **canon** is a particular type of imitation. It is like a **round**, where the imitating voice or instrumental part repeats the entire melody, not just the opening. Of course, as in a round, several voices or instrumental parts might be involved in the canon.

Activity

3 Try singing through a round or a canon in a group. Although you all sing the same part, everyone starts at a different time. However, it all fits together! Try to work out how this happens.

Layered texture

This means that the music is made up of different 'layers' of sound, which are all important in adding to the rich texture of the music. These could be different rhythmic as well as melodic musical lines. Layered texture is a feature of African music as well as gamelan and modern music.

Unison, octaves, single line melody

Unison is all the instruments or voices playing or singing notes at the same pitch. If the instruments or parts play or sing notes an octave apart, this is called **octaves**. To be in unison, the notes must be at the same pitch.

A single line melody is an example of a **monophonic** texture. As the name suggests, this is a single melody line without any harmonies, although it may be played by more than one instrument or voice.

Antiphonal

This is a special kind of imitation where a musical phrase is tossed between different groups of voices or instruments. In some antiphonal music the instruments or voices are placed in different parts of the building, or on different sides of a concert platform. This produces a kind of stereo or quadrophonic effect as a musical phrase is passed from one group to another.

AQA Examiner's tip

When trying to work out whether the texture is harmonic/homophonic or polyphonic/contrapuntal, listen out for the melody and overall effect. If there is a clear melody supported by some kind of chordal accompaniment, then it is a harmonic/homophonic texture. If the texture sounds 'busy', with melodies weaving in and out of each other, this is a polyphonic/contrapuntal texture.

Did you know ??????

A canon is an example of a polyphonic/contrapuntal texture, because all the parts involved in the canon are of equal importance, are interwoven, and fit together harmonically.

Did you know ??????

Italian church composers around the turn of the 17th century particularly loved writing antiphonal music. They placed groups of singers and instrumentalists in different galleries in the church, producing spectacular spatial effects.

2.7 Texture and melody

What is meant by 'melody'

A **melody** is a rhythmically organised pattern of single notes arranged in succession, one after the other. In melody the notes are arranged horizontally (whereas in harmony they are arranged vertically).

What will you need to learn?

You will need to recognise the following melodic features:

- intervals within the octave
- conjunct, disjunct, triadic, scalic, arpeggio
- passing notes, acciaccaturas, appoggiaturas
- blue notes
- diatonic, chromatic, pentatonic, whole tone, modal
- augmentation, diminution, sequence, inversion
- slide/glissando/portamento, ornamentation
- ostinato, riff
- phrasing, articulation
- pitch bend
- improvisation.

Intervals within the octave

We have already learned the names given to the different notes, called the **degrees of a scale**, in the section on harmony (see page 20).

The distance in pitch between two different notes in a scale is called an **interval**. The two notes may be sounded together, or one after the other. An interval is identified by counting the distance in pitch between the two notes. This includes counting the bottom and top notes, and the number of lines and spaces between them. For example, the distance between the notes C and G is a 5th, since the interval covers the notes C, D, E, F and G.

Intervals within the octave

2nd 3rd 4th 5th 6th 7th Octave

A

Conjunct, disjunct, triadic, scalic, arpeggio

These are all different kinds of melodic note patterns. **Conjunct** means that the notes in the melody move mainly by step: in other words, they are mostly next to each other in pitch. A **disjunct** melody moves mainly by leaps (wide intervals between the notes). A **triadic** melody begins by using notes that belong to a triad (three-note chord), often the tonic triad of the piece. This is very useful in establishing the key and tonality of a piece. A **scalic** melody is made up of notes that follow the order of a particular scale.

An **arpeggio** is a type of broken chord, where the notes are played one after the other, either going up (ascending) or going down (descending). It is sometimes called a 'spread' chord, and the pattern of notes can cover one or more octaves. It is sometimes indicated by putting a wiggly line in front of the notes of a chord to show that they are to be played one after the other. Arpeggios can be both a melodic and a harmonic feature.

Arpeggio

Passing notes, acciaccaturas, appoggiaturas

A **passing note** is a note in a melody that connects two notes that are part of the harmony. For example, in a melody you might have C followed by E; these two notes are recognisable as part of the chord of C major. To smooth out the melodic line between these notes, the note D might be added in between them. This note does not belong to the chord of C major, but is a passing note, since it 'passes' between the two 'harmony' notes. Passing notes usually, but not always, occur on weak beats. For example:

passing note   passing note

The **acciaccatura** and **appoggiatura** are ornaments, which means they are used to decorate or embellish a note in some way. They are often written as very small notes in the printed music. An acciaccatura is shown as a ♪ in the music. It is played a tone or a semitone above or below the melody note it is decorating. It is sometimes called a 'crushed' note because it is played very quickly before the melody note:

written   played

An appoggiatura looks similar to an acciaccatura, but without the line through it. It is given its full value:

written   played

> ### Did you know ??????
> *Appoggiatura* literally means 'leaning' note, because it sounds as if it is leaning on the melody note that follows.

2.8 Texture and melody

Blue notes

These are special notes which are used in blues music. In the melody, some notes are played a semitone lower. For example, if a melody is based on the notes of the chord of C major – C, E, G – the melody might change the note E to an E♭. The scale of C major, with blue notes, might look something like:

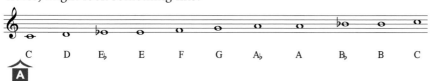

C   D   E♭   E   F   G   A♭   A   B♭   B   C

A

When blue notes appear in the melody, blues performers often 'slide' from one to the other:

B

Diatonic, chromatic, pentatonic, whole tone, modal

These terms can all be used to describe a melody. We have learnt about the terms **diatonic**, **chromatic** and **modal** in the section on harmony and tonality (see pages 18–23).

Pentatonic scales have five different pitches within the octave. Their characteristic sound is often heard in Celtic folk melodies, and those of Africa and East Asia.

A **whole tone** scale consists of exactly what it describes – whole tones. Unlike a major or minor scale, there are no semitones. Here is a whole tone scale starting on C:

C   D   E   F♯   G♯   A♯   C

C

Augmentation, diminution, sequence, inversion

Augmentation and **diminution** have already been learnt in the section on rhythm and metre (see pages 14–17).

A **sequence** is where a melodic phrase is immediately repeated at a different pitch, often by step. If the sequence gets higher in pitch it is called an **ascending sequence**. Alternatively, the pitch may get progressively lower, in which case it is a **descending sequence**.

An **inversion** is where a tune is turned 'upside down' so that the intervals between the notes which rise in the original version now fall, and vice versa.

original   inversion

D

Objectives

You will learn:

more about texture and melody.

Key terms

Diatonic: melody uses only notes that belong to the scale or key that the music is written in.

Chromatic: melody uses some notes that do not belong to the scale.

Modal: modes are ancient scales. A distinctive feature may be a tone between the 7th and 8th notes of the scale.

Augmentation: where a melody or series of notes is drawn out by using notes of a longer duration.

Diminution: where the note lengths of the original melody have been shortened when it is played again.

Dissonance: a musical 'clash'.

Activity

1   Improvise a piece using the pentatonic scale C, D, E, G, A. Play or sing it together with a different pentatonic melody made up by a friend using the same notes. You will find that the contrapuntal texture works. This is because the pentatonic scale has no semitones to cause a **dissonance** when the melodies are played together.

Slide/glissando/portamento

These terms describe the same melodic device: sliding from one note to another. On some instruments, for instance piano or harp, it means playing all the notes in between, by sliding the fingers quickly over keys or strings. A good example of a glissando can be heard played by the clarinet in the opening of George Gershwin's *Rhapsody in Blue*.

Ornamentation

Ornamentation is the decoration or embellishment of the melodic line. As well as the acciaccatura and appoggiatura discussed earlier, some of the most common ornaments are the **trill**, the **turn** and the **mordent**.

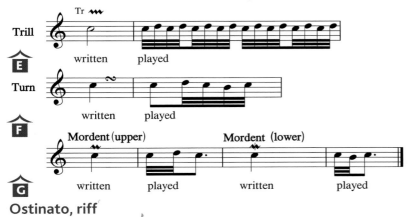

Ostinato, riff

An **ostinato** is a short rhythmic or melodic phrase or pattern that is repeated a number of times in succession. The term **riff** means the same thing, but is usually used in popular music.

Phrasing, articulation

These concern the way the music is performed.

- **Legato**: the notes of the melody should be played smoothly.
- **Staccato**: the notes should be played short and detached. This is indicated by dots above or below the note heads.
- **Slur**: a curved line over a passage of music indicates that it should be played in a smooth, unbroken legato style.
- *Sforzando*: a sudden strong accent in the music. It is shown by the sign *sf*, *sfz* or *fz*.

Pitch bend

This is when a note is raised or lowered in pitch slightly. This is often used in guitar technique, although it can be produced on any string instrument, vocally or on a synthesiser, for example.

Improvisation

This is where a musician invents new musical ideas on the spot, during a performance. It is a feature of much modern music, jazz, and also Indian classical music. When improvising, performers often develop features of the music such as chord patterns, rhythms and melodic phrases. Improvisations display the performer's **virtuoso** skills by being fast or technically difficult.

Activity

2   Bring in some recordings of riffs in popular music. Play them to the class and discuss why they are so memorable.

AQA *Examiner's tip*

Try to listen to recordings or performances of these ornaments so that you become familiar with what they sound like.

Key terms

Virtuoso: a musician who has, or displays, outstanding technical ability.

2.9 Timbre and dynamics

What is meant by 'timbre'

Timbre is the characteristic individual sound or tone-colour of an instrument or voice. It is what enables us to tell the difference between, say, a violin, a trumpet and a flute – even if they all play the same note.

Many factors account for this: for example, the materials from which the instrument is made, the way it produces its sound (for example with strings, or with a reed) and the way the sound is made to resonate (such as in the hollow body of a string instrument). When an instrument plays a note, something vibrates – for instance a string, or the air inside a length of tube. The vibrations act in a complicated way: the note we hear most strongly is called the **fundamental**, and this is the note we think of as being played, but added to that are fainter, higher notes called **harmonics** or **overtones**. These add 'colour' to the fundamental. Some instruments produce more harmonics than others, or emphasise different harmonics. It is the relative strengths of the harmonics, and the way they are combined, that gives instruments and voices their unique, distinctive timbre.

Timbre is important to a composer because it adds a special quality to the music which helps to create mood or feeling. Composers may use instruments on their own (solo), or blend together the timbres of several instruments to produce a particular effect. In the examination you may be asked to recognise individual instruments, or groups of instruments, or to comment in some way on the effect created in the music by using particular instruments or combinations of instruments.

A *Saxophonists*

What will you need to learn?

You will need to be able to recognise the following:

- instruments and voices, singly and in combination, as found in music for solo instruments, concertos, chamber groups, pop and vocal music
- generic families of instruments, as found in world music
- timbre, including the use of technology, synthesised and computer-generated sounds, sampling, and the use of techniques such as reverb, distortion and chorus
- instrumental techniques including *con arco* (with a bow), *pizzicato* (plucked), *con sordino* (muted), double-stopping, and *tremolo/ tremolando*
- vocal techniques such as *falsetto and vibrato*.

In the examination, recognition of individual instruments and groups of instruments will be based on excerpts taken from the three Strands of Learning (see page 13).

The individual instruments and instrumental groups will be covered in Chapters 3–5. However, you should try to develop your recognition of different instruments, instrumental sections (e.g. brass, strings) and different combinations of instruments by listening to many kinds of music.

B *Paul Simon performs on stage to promote his Graceland tour*

2.10 Timbre and dynamics

The use of technology

Technology has enabled instruments not only to change their sound, but also to produce instrumental sounds that are created electronically. You may be asked to recognise some technology-based timbres:

- **Reverb** – an abbreviation of **reverberation**. This is when a sound lasts longer because it is reflected between the walls, floor and ceiling of a room. It can be created electronically, or added to an *acoustic* (non-electronic) sound to improve the tone-quality.

- **Distortion** is often used in rock music, particularly on the electric guitar, sometimes creating an aggressive sound.

- **Chorus** is when a recorded voice or instrument is multiplied electronically, producing the effect of one voice or instrument sounding like many.

- **Multi-tracking** is a recording technique in which different tracks of sound are recorded separately but can be played back together. This enables one performer to play or sing the different parts, combining them on playback.

- **Compression** boosts the level of the quietest sounds in a piece of music, so that they balance with the louder sounds. This creates a more balanced dynamic level, giving an overall impression of an increase in volume, but without the louder sounds dominating.

- A **vocoder** is essentially a device for synthesising speech. It works by electronically combining the characteristics of a human voice with a musical instrument.

- A **sequencer** is an electronic device or computer program that is used to record, edit and play back music data using **MIDI**.

- **Panning** occurs when the sound is electronically moved across from one speaker to another, or is separated into different speakers.

Did you know ??????

Synthesisers can produce special electronic sound effects, but at the touch of a button a single performer can choose from an amazing variety of **samples** of different individual instrumental sounds, sections or groups – or even a whole orchestra!

Listening activity

1. Listen to examples of the electronic effects listed here, so that you become familiar with how they sound. You might be able to do this by visiting your school's or a local recording studio.

Key terms

Synthesiser: an electronic instrument, usually a keyboard, which can combine waveforms to imitate the sounds of other instruments.

Sample: an electronic recording of a sound that can then be reproduced at any pitch, using a keyboard.

MIDI: Musical Instrumental Digital Interface – a system which enables performance data to be exchanged between suitably equipped computers and instruments (such as keyboards), and enables complex compositions to be built up a part at a time.

A *Using a synthesiser*

Instrumental techniques

These are particular ways of playing an instrument that can affect and enhance its timbre.

In the examination you may be required to recognise the following techniques:

- **Con arco**. This means playing a string instrument such as a violin, viola, cello or double bass with a bow.
- **Pizzicato**. This is where the strings are plucked instead of played with a bow.
- **Con sordino**. This means 'with a mute'. On string instruments the mute is a device attached to the bridge (the part which raises the strings above the body of the instrument), dampening the vibrations to produce a softer sound. On brass instruments there are different kinds of mutes that produce a variety of effects. These are placed inside the bell of the instrument (where the sound comes out).
- **Double-stopping**. This is where string players bow two notes simultaneously, on adjacent strings. In triple- or quadruple-stopping, three or four notes are played. It sounds like a chord (although the player actually plays the lower strings first and then rocks the bow to play the higher strings in quick succession, since the curve of the bridge prevents all the strings from being played at the same time).
- **Tremolo/tremolando**. Another string effect, this literally means 'trembling' or 'quivering'. It is produced by rapid up-and-down movements of the bow on the strings, creating an agitated, shimmering effect.

Vocal techniques

- **Falsetto** is a technique employed by male singers, to enable them to sing notes higher than their normal range.

> **Listening activity**
>
> 3   Listen to 'Olin lacus colueram' from the cantata *Carmina Burana* by Carl Orff (CD track 1). *Carmina Burana* (composed in 1935–6) is based on 24 poems taken from a collection written in Latin during the 13th century. 'Olin lacus colueram' is about a swan, once proud and beautiful, but now being roasted on a spit to be served up as dinner. The song is sung by a tenor, but to emphasise the bitterness and agony of the swan, Orff writes the music very high, above the tenor's normal vocal range. This produces the strained, weak tone called **falsetto** (see above).

- **Vibrato**. This technique literally means 'quivering' or 'shaking', and is an effect caused by small and rapid changes to the pitch of a note. It is used by string players and singers to add warmth and expression to the tone of the music.

> **Listening activity**
>
> 2   Listen to the effect of mutes on brass instruments, either by listening to recordings or by finding a brass player in your school who can demonstrate them to you.

> **Did you know ??????**
>
> Falsetto singing can be found in many different kinds of music, including popular music styles such as 'doo wop'.

Timbre and dynamics

Dynamics

Dynamics are the varying levels of loudness or softness in a piece of music. They are indicated by letters, signs, abbreviations or symbols in the music. Dynamics may change suddenly, or gradually, over a few notes or bars.

In the examination you may be asked to comment on the dynamic level in an excerpt by identifying or using the appropriate signs, terms and symbols.

Common signs, terms and symbols

Two basic dynamic indications are used in music. These are:

- **p**, which is the first letter of the Italian word *piano*, which means 'soft'
- **f**, which is the first letter of the Italian word *forte*, which means 'loud' or 'strong'.

To indicate more extreme levels, more of the same letter are added. For example:

- **f** – loud (*forte*)
- **ff** – very loud (*fortissimo*)
- **fff** – extremely loud (*fortissississimo*)

or, at the other extreme:

- **p** – soft (*piano*)
- **pp** – very soft (*pianissimo*)
- **ppp** – extremely soft (*pianississimo*).

Most pieces of music do not go beyond three letters to indicate extreme dynamics. However, there are some examples of composers using four, five, and even six **p**s or **f**s in their music!

More subtle shades of dynamics, those between soft and loud, are indicated by:

- **mp** – moderately soft (*mezzo piano*)
- **mf** – moderately loud (*mezzo forte*).

Dynamic levels are relative to each other. Unlike tempo, which can be given a precise indication using a metronome, there is no way of indicating exactly how loud or soft a piece should be. This is left to the performer, who will take into consideration factors such as the size of the room the performance is taking place in.

Objectives

You will learn:

what is meant by 'dynamics'

about the different elements which make up this area.

Key terms

Dynamics: the varying levels of loudness or softness in a piece of music.

Listening activity

Listen to a recording or live performance of the slow movement from Haydn's Symphony No. 94 in G. This is nicknamed the 'Surprise' Symphony, because shortly after the opening of the second movement, after the theme has been heard twice (the first time *piano*, and the second time even softer, *pianissimo*), there is a sudden loud, *fortissimo* chord. This was one of Haydn's famous jokes. It was intended to 'make all the ladies jump', and must have created quite a stir at the time. It is a good example of a sudden dynamic change – but does it really make you jump? Is our world so much noisier than Haydn's that we need greater dynamic contrasts to achieve the same effect?

Other commonly used signs are:

- *fp* – loud, then suddenly soft (*forte-piano*)
- *fz* (*forzato*), *sf*, or *sfz* (*sforzando*) – suddenly forcing or accenting a note
- *sfp* – forcing or accenting a note followed immediately by *piano*.

Gradual changes

The two most common gradual changes in dynamics are:

- **crescendo** (getting louder)
- **decrescendo** or **diminuendo** (getting softer)

These terms, like the letters discussed previously, are usually indicated below the stave. Crescendo is often shortened to **cresc.**, decrescendo to **decresc.**, and diminuendo to **dim**.

For quicker changes the word **molto** ('more' or 'much') is often used, for example *molto cresc.* or *molto dim.* For slower changes the words **poco a poco** (little by little) are often used, as in *poco a poco cresc.* Dashes may be used to show exactly how long a *crescendo* or *diminuendo* should last, for example *cresc.* _ _ _ _ _ _ _ _ _ _

Another way of indicating gradual changes in dynamics is by using 'hairpins', so called because they look like old-fashioned hairpins. They are used to indicate quicker changes in dynamics, usually over a bar or two.

- ⊂ – this means the dynamic level gets louder.
- ⊃ – this means the dynamic level gets softer.

2.12 Structure and form

Structure and form are words that are used to describe the way musical ideas are arranged and ordered in a composition. In most pieces of music, this is concerned with how a composer balances **repetition** and **contrast**. Repetition of previous musical material is useful in creating a sense of unity within a piece, although too much repetition can result in the music becoming predictable and boring. There are many ways in which contrasts or changes to the music can be introduced – for example, the introduction of a new melody, a new key, or different harmonies or instrumentation. This adds variety and interest, but too much contrast may make the music seem confusing and lacking in shape.

It is usual to identify the different sections in a piece of music by using letter names, so that the opening section would be called A, and each new, contrasting section would be given a different letter name. If a section is repeated, it has the same letter name as when it was first heard: for example, A2 would be the first repeat of section A.

What will you need to learn?

You will need to learn the following structures and forms, and be able to recognise them in short musical excerpts. Some structures, such as sonata form for example, are too long to be tested in the examination. However, you should try to become familiar with all of the structures and forms dealt with in this section, as it will help you understand much of the music you may study in the Strands of Learning.

- binary, ternary, call and response
- rondo, theme and variations, arch-shape
- sonata, minuet and trio, scherzo and trio
- strophic, through-composed, da capo aria, cyclic
- popular song forms
- ground bass, continuo, cadenza.

Binary, ternary, call and response

A piece that is in **binary** form has two sections of roughly equal length. The first section (A) is answered by the second section (B). Each section is usually repeated.

There is also usually a change of key, or **modulation** during Section A, so that it ends in a new key. If the piece is in a major key this is most likely to be the **dominant** (see page 20). In minor keys the modulation is typically to the **relative major** (see page 22), although it may end with an **imperfect cadence** (see page 20). The second section of the piece (B) begins in the new key, but will eventually modulate back to the original, **tonic** key.

Ternary form is built up in three sections, A B A:

A1	B	A2

Section B contains music that contrasts with Section A in some way. The repeat of section A (A2) can be exactly the same as the original, or the composer may have changed some details to make it more interesting than listening to a straight repeat.

Call and response is where a musical phrase that is played or sung by one musician, is immediately followed by a responding phrase from another musician or the whole group. It is common in traditional African music, and in African-American music such as spirituals, gospel, blues and jazz.

AQA *Examiner's tip*

In the examination, you may be asked to recognise the form or structure of an excerpt of music either by selecting the correct answer from a multiple choice list, or by writing your own answer using letters (e.g. ABA) or the name of the form (ternary). Try to listen for changes in the music, such as a new melody, which tell you that a new section has begun. Listen for any repeats of music you have already heard.

C *African singers*

Rondo, theme and variations, arch-shape

The word *rondo* is taken from a Latin word which means 'to return', and that is exactly what happens in the music. The main theme (A) keeps on returning, with contrasting sections of music in between. These contrasting sections are called **episodes**. Rondo is an example of a multi-sectional form, since it has more sections than binary or ternary form.

Here is an example of a rondo form that has two contrasting episodes, although it is not unusual to find rondos that have three, four or even more episodes.

A1 (main theme)	B1 (first episode)	A2 (repeat of main theme)	C (second episode)	A3 (repeat of main theme)	B2 (repeat of first episode)	A4 (repeat of main theme)

A

Of course, as previously mentioned, a composer may change the repeats of the main theme in some way (often by making them shorter), since it 'returns' a number of times.

Theme and variations form involves starting a piece of music with a theme, and then repeating the theme a number of times, but changing, or 'varying' it each time. The opening theme is usually easy to remember, and often in binary or ternary form.

Activities

1. As a group or class, find a well-known tune and each have a go at composing a variation on it. Think about what features of the original tune you might develop in your variation, and how you are going to change it. Perform your music, starting with the theme and then, in turn, each person's variation. Discuss how each has developed or altered the original theme.

2. Listen to a recording of Mozart's variations on 'Ah vous dirai-je, maman'. You will recognise the theme as the melody 'Twinkle, twinkle, little star'. Discuss how Mozart develops and changes the opening theme in his variations.

Arch-shape is a type of form or structure which is symmetrical, so that the plan of the music resembles the shape of an arch: for example, ABCBA.

Did you know ??????

Many themes used by composers for their theme and variations pieces were not written by the composers themselves, but were well-known tunes, perhaps taken from an opera that was popular at the time. Each variation alters or develops features found in the original theme, perhaps by changing the tempo, rhythm, harmony, tonality (particularly from major to minor or vice versa) or by embellishing the music with scale-like passages or ornaments. Theme and variations form was often used by composers to show how inventive and ingenious they could be in developing musical ideas from a simple opening theme.

B

Sonata form

Sonata form is a large-scale musical form, too long to be tested aurally through musical excerpts in the examination. The sonata as a **genre** is dealt with in Chapter 3. Basically, sonata form consists of three main sections called the **exposition**, **development** and **recapitulation**.

Sonata form is like a three-act play. The characters (subjects) are introduced in the exposition. They go through all sorts of dramatic situations in the development, and then everything is sorted out and resolved in the recapitulation.

> **Key terms**
>
> **Genre:** a category or type (here, of music).

C

Exposition	Development	Recapitulation
First subject (tonic)	Lots of key changes; musical ideas from the exposition are developed.	First subject (tonic)
Bridge passage (modulates)		Bridge passage (altered)
Second subject (new key)		Second subject (tonic)
Codetta (section ends in new key)		Coda (rounding off)

In the **exposition**, the composer 'expounds' or presents the main musical ideas, called 'subjects'. A subject is typically a melodic idea, and there are usually two of them in the exposition. The **first subject** is in the tonic key and the **second subject** contrasts by being in a different key (usually the dominant in a major key, or the relative major in a minor key) and mood. The two subjects are linked by a **bridge passage**, a section in which the music modulates from the first to the second subject. The bridge passage often uses scale-like passages, because scales are good at defining the key of the music. The exposition may be 'rounded off' by a short **codetta**, and ends in the new key.

The **development** section develops ideas such as melodic phrases or rhythms found in the exposition. It is a dramatic section in the piece, usually with lots of key changes.

The **recapitulation** brings back the musical ideas from the exposition, but with the bridge passage altered so that the second subject returns in the tonic key. The whole movement may be rounded off by a **coda**, which is a longer version of the codetta found at the end of the exposition.

Be aware, however, that there are many different versions of the basic outline given above. A slow introduction may precede the exposition, for example, and there may be more than one 'second subject', so don't expect every sonata form to follow exactly the same plan. As in theme and variation form, composers like to show how inventive they can be.

Minuet and trio

A minuet is a dance that was popular during the 17th and 18th centuries, particularly in the royal courts. It is a stately dance, in 3/4 time, performed at a moderate tempo.

In **minuet and trio form**, the trio forms the middle section (B) of a ternary (ABA) structure, followed by a repeat of the minuet (A). The trio has a thinner texture: often there were just three parts (hence the name 'trio'), though this is not always the case. Within the overall ternary form, the individual sections (the minuet and the trio) are in binary form.

A1 Minuet 1	**B** Trio	**A2** Minuet 1
	Contrasting tune, key and texture	Repeat of minuet, but without internal repeats
‖: a :‖: b :‖	‖: c :‖: d :‖	| a | b ‖

Strophic, through-composed, **da capo aria**

These are all forms used in vocal music. **Strophic** form is when the same music is repeated for different verses in a song. A good example can be found in most hymn tunes.

Through-composed is the opposite of strophic, with new music for each verse in a song. The music develops continuously, changing to reflect different moods or situations described in the text.

A **da capo aria** is a type of song found frequently in opera. *Aria* literally means 'air' – another word for a melody. In an opera it is sung by a solo singer with an orchestral accompaniment.

Cyclic form

Unlike most other forms looked at so far, where there is progression from one section to another, cyclic form is the constant repetition of a fixed number of beats, or melodic pattern. During each cycle, rhythms or melodic patterns can be repeated and developed through improvisation, or by changes in texture or dynamics. Cyclic music is common in Africa, India and Asia – for example, Indonesian gamelan music.

Objectives

You will learn:

about minuet and trio forms

about song forms and ground bass.

Remember

The trio is actually another minuet since it is in 3/4 and has a binary structure with both sections repeated. Compared with the minuet, it is quieter and in a contrasting key (again, usually the dominant or, if the minuet was in a minor key, the relative major).

Did you know ??????

During the Classical period in music (around 1750 to 1810), the minuet and trio became popular in instrumental music that was intended for listening rather than dancing. The **scherzo and trio** follows the same form, but is more energetic. The word scherzo means 'a joke'.

Popular song forms

There are many different kinds of forms used in popular song (see page 67). In the examination you may be asked to recognise the structure of a piece of popular music by using letters or the name of the form. One common structure of popular song is built around **verse** and **chorus**, which have contrasting music. Other features may include an **intro** (introduction), an **outro** (a coda, or rounding off after the final verse or chorus), and **fills**, which are a bridge between the sections, often supplied by the guitar (guitar fill) or drums (drum fill).

A classic example of a popular music form is the **12-bar blues** (see page 63).

Activity

Try playing the 12-bar blues structure, then play, sing or listen to different types of popular music. Try to work out the form using letter names. Try to identify the verse and chorus, and whether the music has an intro and outro. What kind of fills are used in the music?

Ground bass

A **ground bass** is a melody in the bass (lowest part) that is repeated throughout the music. While the bass line is repeated, the melody and sometimes the harmony keep changing, so that the repeated ground bass unifies the whole piece while providing the basis for melodic and/ or harmonic variations. There are many examples in all kinds of music (see page 49 for a ground bass used in baroque music). In popular music, a ground bass could be a riff that is repeated continuously throughout a piece of music while the accompanying melody and harmony keep changing, for example in 'Money' from Pink Floyd's *Dark Side of the Moon*.

B *Pink Floyd's bassist*

Remember

A *da capo* aria is in ternary form. An opening section (A) is followed by a contrasting section (B), which might differ in melody, key, instrumentation, texture, mood, and so on. In the score, at the end of the B section the letters D.C. are written. This is short for *da capo*, which means 'from the head', telling the performers to go back to the start of the music (section A). After this repeat, at the end of section A, the word *fine* (end) is written in the music, showing the performers where to finish.

Remember

In popular song forms, the chorus is sometimes called the *refrain*. It is the focal point of the song, often remembered for its catchy tune and often emphasised by a fuller instrumentation. The *lyrics* (words) are usually the same for each repetition of the chorus.

The verse is the part of the song where the story-line is told. The music may be repeated for each verse, but the words change and the music is less prominent.

The three Strands of Learning are broad categories of music from which all of the musical excerpts in the listening examination will be taken. They are:

- the Western Classical tradition
- popular music of the 20th and 21st centuries
- world music.

Within each strand there are a number of specific areas and genres from which all of the musical excerpts contained on the CD in the examination will be taken. It is by exploring music from these areas that you will be able to understand and recognise the elements of music listed in the five Areas of Study and gain an appreciation of how composers have used the Areas of Study, in different kinds of music. The areas and genres to explore within the three strands are:

The Western Classical tradition

- Baroque orchestral music
- The concerto
- Music for voices
- Chamber music
- The sonata

Popular music of the 20th and 21st centuries

- Blues
- Popular music of the 1960s
- Rock music, R'n'B (rhythm and bass), hip-hop
- Music theatre
- Film music

World music

- Music of the Caribbean
- Music of Africa
- Music of India

In the listening examination you will not be tested on your knowledge of any of the specific areas or genres listed above. Questions will focus on being able to recognise and respond to features related to the five Areas of Study.

Objectives

You will learn:

about the three Strands of Learning

about the different areas and genres that make up each strand

how these will be tested in the listening examination

how they link with the composition units.

Types of question

In the examination, questions will be of three different types. These are:

- objective tests
- structured responses
- extended responses.

Objective tests require single-word answers. For example, you might be asked to identify a particular feature in an instrumental part, such as a riff.

Structured responses are answers that are linked to a particular area (tonality, dynamics and so on) and you might have to choose an answer from a multiple-choice list. For example:

> *Which word best describes the tonality of this excerpt?*

> *Circle your answer.*

> *major   minor   modal   pentatonic*

Activity

Chapters 3–5 will cover the areas and genres contained within the three Strands of Learning. However, you should try to develop your knowledge of these areas further by listening to as many examples as possible, not only to try to recognise features and devices contained in the five Areas of Study, but also to become familiar with how composers have used these features in their music, and the characteristics of the different genres, which will also help you in the composition units.

Extended responses enable you to respond in a fuller, more extended manner. Open-ended questions, such as 'What effect does this have on the music?' or 'Give a reason for your choice' require extended responses.

How the Strands of Learning link with composing

For Unit 2 you will be required to compose one piece of music. This composition must explore *two or more* of the five Areas of Study, and also be linked to *one* of the three Strands of Learning, as announced annually by AQA.

For Unit 4 you will be required to compose *one* piece of music that explores *two or more* of the five Areas of Study, but this may be in any style or genre.

There is more information about the composition units in chapters 6–10.

2

In this chapter you have learnt:

✔ about the five Areas of Study

✔ what is meant by rhythm and metre

✔ what is meant by harmony and tonality

✔ what is meant by texture and melody

✔ what is meant by timbre and dynamics

✔ what is meant by structure and form

✔ about the different musical elements that make up each area of study

✔ how these will be tested in the listening examination

✔ about the three Strands of Learning

✔ about the specific areas and genres that make up the three Strands of Learning

✔ how the five Areas of Study and three Strands of Learning relate to each other and the composing units

✔ about the different question types used in the listening examination.

Revision quiz

Try answering the following questions without looking back over the chapter. The answers can be found on page 180.

1 What is meant by rhythm and metre?

2 What is a polyrhythm?

3 What is meant by rubato?

4 What is meant by a drone?

5 Which two chords make up a perfect cadence?

6 What term is used to describe a change from one key to another?

7 Describe a harmonic/homophonic texture.

8 Describe a polyphonic/contrapuntal texture.

9 What are blue notes?

10 What is an ostinato or riff?

11 What is a sequence?

12 What term describes a melodic line that moves mainly by step?

13 What is an appoggiatura?

14 What is meant by the term 'pizzicato'?

15 What term is used to describe a gradual increase in the dynamic level of a passage of music?

3 The Western Classical tradition

Introduction

In this chapter you will learn about the first of the three Strands of Learning and the specific areas and genres that form the focus for this strand. Although the musical excerpts contained on the CD in the examination will be taken from these genres, your knowledge of them – as genres – will not be tested in the examination. It is by exploring music from these areas that you will be able to understand and recognise the elements of music listed in the five Areas of Study, and gain an appreciation of how composers have used these in different kinds of music. This chapter will provide you with a background to the different areas and genres, but will focus on how they may illustrate the terms and devices covered in the five Areas of Study.

This chapter will cover the 'Western Classical tradition' Strand of Learning, and the specific areas and genres that form the focus of this strand:

- Baroque orchestral music
- The concerto
- Music for voices
- Chamber music
- The sonata.

3.1 The baroque orchestra

What is meant by the 'Western Classical tradition'

This term is used to refer to music that has developed in Western countries (for example, Italy or Germany) over many centuries. The term 'classical', in its broadest form, is often used to describe music that is not related to various kinds of modern popular music.

Baroque orchestral music

The term **baroque** is applied to music composed between about 1600 (when the first operas were composed) and 1750 (the death of one of the greatest baroque composers, J. S. Bach). The term comes from a Portuguese word, *barocca*, meaning an irregular shaped pearl set in a piece of elaborate jewellery. This seems an odd term to apply to a style of music, but music written during this period, like the art and architecture, could be very ornamented and elaborate. **Polyphonic/ contrapuntal** textures are very common.

It was during the baroque period that the orchestra started to take shape, and there were many developments in instruments: for example, violins replaced the weaker sounding viols, and flutes gradually replaced recorders. The foundation of a typical baroque orchestra was the strings, particularly the violins. The other sections (woodwind, brass and percussion) were not yet standardised, and varied from piece to piece.

A *Santa Cecilia concert hall, Rome*

Brass instruments did not possess valves, and so were limited in the notes they could play in their range. A typical feature of baroque trumpet parts is that they often play tunes that are very high. Without valves, these *natural* trumpets could only produce notes of a different pitch when the player changed his *embouchure*, or lip pressure. This did not produce a full range of notes, as on a modern trumpet, but restricted the player to the **harmonic series** (see page 30). The lower notes of the harmonic series are widely spaced, but higher in the range the notes are closer together, and are more suitable for playing melodies.

Woodwind (without clarinets, which had not been invented) and percussion instruments were used less often. A common feature of the baroque orchestra was the continuo. This is where a chord-playing instrument, usually a keyboard instrument such as a harpsichord, plays a part based on the bass line and harmonies of the piece. If you listen carefully to a recording of baroque orchestral music you will hear the characteristic sound of the harpsichord accompanying the orchestral texture.

Did you know ??????

Important baroque composers include:

- Monteverdi (1567–1643)
- Domenico Scarlatti (1685–1757)
- Vivaldi (1678–1741)
- Corelli (1653–1713)
- Purcell (c.1659–1695)
- Couperin (1668–1733)
- Rameau (1683–1764)
- Lully (1632–1687)
- J. S. Bach (1685–1750)
- Handel (1685–1759)

Activities

1   Find out more about the harmonic series. Your science teacher may help explain what happens. What notes were available on a 'natural' trumpet? Listen to recordings of baroque music using natural trumpets playing high in their range. Does this create a particular effect in the music? Can you think of any reasons why baroque composers might not use brass instruments, such as the trumpet, in every piece of orchestral music?

2   Do some research on the composers listed here by using your music department's resources and the internet. Try to listen to some music by each of these composers. Do you notice any similarities in their use of instruments or textures?

B *Harpsichord*

3.2 Baroque genres

The suite

A suite is a collection of dances. Many suites were written by baroque composers for the harpsichord or orchestra. The different dances in a suite were usually in the same key, and in binary form.

A piece in binary form has two sections of roughly equal length. The first section (A), is answered by the second section (B). Usually, each section is repeated.

French composers often included dances in rondo form, which is a multi-sectional form, e.g. ABACADA (see page 38).

A popular dance during the baroque period was the minuet. This is a stately dance in 3/4 time (see page 40). A minuet is in binary (AB) form, but often two different minuets (usually contrasting in key) were played one after the other, with the first minuet repeated at the end to form an overall ABA (ternary form) structure.

A1	B	A2
Minuet 1	Minuet 2	Minuet 1

‖: a :‖: b :‖   ‖: c :‖: d :‖ | a | b ‖

A

The concerto

A concerto is an instrumental composition that features a soloist (or small group of soloists) contrasted against a larger group of accompanying instruments (an orchestra). This was a popular genre with baroque composers, because it gave them the opportunity to contrast dynamics and instrumental timbres between the solo instrument (or group) and the fuller sound produced by the larger, accompanying group of instruments.

There were many types of concertos in the baroque period, with different numbers of solo instruments, but the two most popular types were the **solo concerto**, and the **concerto grosso**. The solo concerto has one instrument (the solo) contrasted against a larger group. A concerto grosso ('great concerto') has a small group of solo instruments, called the **concertino**, contrasted against a larger, accompanying group, called the **ripieno**. In both types of concerto it is usual to begin with all the instruments playing the music together. This is called a **tutti**. After that, there are alternating solo **episodes** interspersed with the orchestra playing short repeated versions of the opening tutti.

Objectives

You will learn:

what is meant by 'suite'

what is meant by 'solo concerto' and 'concerto grosso'

what is meant by 'ground bass'.

Listening activity

1 Listen to two minuets from Handel's *Music for the Royal Fireworks* (CD track 2). Each minuet is in **binary** form, with both the A and B sections repeated. In both minuets there is an **imperfect cadence** at the end of the A section in the first minuet. Note the contrasting **tonality** of the two minuets – the first is in a **major** key, the second is **minor**. The first minuet is repeated after the second minuet, making an overall **ternary** form movement, but this time the A and B sections are not repeated. This is common in structures of this sort, though nowadays it is not unusual for all the repeats to be observed.

Quite often in baroque pieces, a movement in a minor key will end on a final chord in the tonic major (for example a piece in G minor will end in G major). This is an example of a *tierce de Picardie* (see page 20).

Listening activities

2 Listen to the opening of J. S. Bach's Brandenburg Concerto no. 2 in F major (CD track 3). At the opening, all the instruments play together (**tutti**), introducing the musical melodies and ideas. After this, instead of a soloist, the instruments that make up the solo group, or **concertino**, are introduced in pairs in between passages of music played by the accompanying group (**ripieno**).

3 Listen to the opening of Pachelbel's *Canon* (CD track4). The ground bass is played first, and then different melodies are added in turn, weaving around each other and the ground bass to produce a rich **contrapuntal** texture. In this piece, each new melody has quicker notes than the previous one. The repeated ground bass does not change, providing an 'anchor' which helps to unify the piece.

4 Listen to the opening of Vivaldi's 'Spring' from *The Four Seasons* (CD track 5). The opening music has all the instruments playing together. This is followed by the solo violin playing a **duet** with another violin. After this the main group of instruments returns, and the excerpt finishes with the solo violin alternating with the other instruments. Listen to the characteristic sound of the harpsichord **continuo** accompanying the orchestra.

■ The ground bass

The use of a ground bass was popular in baroque music. This enabled the composer to achieve unity in the music (because the ground bass was repeated throughout the piece) – but also variety, since new melodies could be added above the ground bass.

Listening quiz

Listen to the opening of J. S. Bach's Brandenburg Concerto no. 2 in F major (CD track 3).

3 After the opening **tutti**, which term best describes the texture when the solo group of instruments play: harmonic/homophonic or polyphonic/contrapuntal?

4 Give a suitable time signature for this excerpt.

5 Name the brass instrument you can hear in this excerpt.

3.3 The concerto

What is meant by 'classical'

When describing music, the word 'classical' is often used in a general way to refer to any music that is not 'pop' music. However, the term also has a more precise meaning, and is used to describe music composed between about 1750 and 1810 (called the 'classical period'). Outside music, the word 'classical' is used to describe the architectural styles of ancient Greece and Rome, with their emphasis on simplicity, line, balance and order. We also use the term to describe something that is of the highest class, which lasts the test of time and can be held up as an example of excellence (e.g. a classic film or car). These descriptions all apply to music of the classical period, with its emphasis on clear melodic lines, homophonic textures and balance of expression and form. The classical period includes the music of Mozart, Haydn and the early compositions of Beethoven.

The classical concerto

In the section on baroque orchestral music (see pages 46–9) we learned about two different kinds of concerto: the solo concerto and the concerto grosso.

During the classical period, the solo concerto, rather than the concerto grosso, gained in popularity. It is in three movements (fast–slow–fast). The first movement is usually the longest, and is in modified **sonata form**. These modifications may include a lengthy introduction that introduces the main themes in an orchestral **tutti**, before the main **exposition** section (often called a 'double exposition' because they both introduce the musical ideas), and the use of solo passages or **episodes**.

Objectives

You will learn:

what is meant by 'classical'

about the classical concerto

about the cadenza

what is meant by 'romantic'

about the romantic concerto

Key terms

Sonata form: this consists of three main sections called the exposition, development and recapitulation (see page 39 for a more detailed explanation).

Listening activity

1. Listen to the opening of Mozart's Clarinet Concerto (CD track 6). The clarinet was a newly invented instrument that Mozart loved, and the concerto demonstrates its different timbres and range, showing off what it can do.

The concerto opens with a lengthy orchestral tutti that introduces the main tunes. The exposition begins when the solo clarinet re-enters with the main tune. Mozart creates a musical dialogue by alternating showy solo passages (accompanied by quiet strings) that decorate or embellish the melodies, which contrast with louder (tutti) orchestral passages.

Cadenza

Towards the end of a movement (usually the first movement, although this could occur in either of the quicker movements) the orchestra pauses, and the soloist plays a showy passage called a **cadenza**. This displays the *virtuosity* or brilliant technique of the soloist. In most classical concertos the cadenza is *improvised*, or made up on the spot, by the soloist. Later on, composers wrote out their own music for

AQA Examiner's tip

Listen to baroque, classical and romantic concertos. Concentrate on identifying devices and terms from the five Areas of Study. You may be asked to recognise whether an excerpt of music is taken from a concerto, so make sure that you can recognise the significant features, such as the cadenza and alternating solo (or solo group) passages with the tutti orchestra. You will not be asked to recognise the period in which the concerto was composed.

the cadenzas. The word *cadenza* means **cadence** (see page 20), and the term is used in a concerto because just before the solo cadenza begins the orchestra pauses on an **imperfect cadence**. This signals the start of the cadenza. A cadenza usually ends with a trill, a signal to the orchestra that the cadenza is about to end, and that they should resume playing.

Listening activity

2   Listen to the third movement of Mozart's Horn Concerto no. 4 in E♭ major (CD track 7). Like many third movements in concertos, it is an example of a **rondo**.

Look at the plan of the movement on this page. Listen for the different sections, and each re-appearance of tune A. Just before the end, the orchestra pauses on an imperfect cadence, and the horn plays the cadenza. After this, theme A returns and the movement is rounded off with a **coda** (see page 38).

Key terms

Rondo: taken from a Latin word which means 'to return': the main theme (A) keeps on returning, with contrasting sections of music in between (see page 38).

A

A	B	A2	C	A3	B2	Cadenza	A	Coda
Horn has the melody first, followed by the orchestra	Horn has the melody first, then in 'conversation' with the orchestra	Horn has the melody first, followed by the orchestra	A new melody in a minor key, played first by the horn. Changes to a major key at the end	Horn has the melody first, followed by the orchestra	A different version of B, but with the soloist and orchestra still in 'discussion'	The orchestra pauses on an imperfect cadence and the horn plays a showy solo	The horn has the melody, followed by the orchestra, which begins the melody before…	… part of the melody is repeated by the horn and the texture builds up to a climax at the end.

Romantic music

The term **Romantic** is applied to music composed between about 1810 and 1910. Whereas classical music aimed to balance expression and form, romantic music placed an emphasis on the expression of emotion and feeling, so that this became the most important aspect of the music. Romantic music is often powerful and intense, expressing the innermost thoughts and feelings of the composers.

Listening activity

3   Listen to the opening of Tchaikovsky's Piano Concerto no. 1 in B♭ minor (CD track 8). It begins with the horns and orchestra introducing the opening notes of the melody. Immediately after this the strings play the melody accompanied by thick piano chords that cover the entire range of the keyboard. The piano then takes over the tune to light **pizzicato** string accompaniment, before it moves into a virtuoso solo passage, full of **chromatic** notes which make it sound improvised, as if it comes 'straight from the heart'. The orchestra then returns with the melody, while the piano accompanies with even richer, more elaborate chords, eventually calming down to a quiet finish. This is a typical romantic concerto – a solo instrument competing with a large orchestra, brilliant technique and showy virtuoso passages from the soloist combined with **dynamic** contrasts and a sense of spontaneity.

Did you know

Important romantic composers:

- The middle and later music of Beethoven (1770–1827)
- Schubert (1797–1828)
- Berlioz (1803–1869)
- Mendelssohn (1809–1847)
- Chopin (1810–1849)
- Schumann (1810–1856)
- Liszt (1811–1886)
- Wagner (1813–1883)
- Verdi (1813–1901)
- Brahms (1833–1897)
- Tchaikovsky (1840–1893)
- Dvořák (1841–1904)
- Grieg (1843–1907)

3.4   Music for voices: choral music

Singing is, perhaps, the oldest musical activity. Singing can take place as a solo activity, in pairs (**duet**) or a small group, a **choir**, accompanied by instruments, or just a voice or voices without any instrumental accompaniment. As with an instrument, the human voice can be trained – but much singing is done by untrained voices. Vocal music has played a long and important role in musical history. It is still one of the most popular activities through which amateur and professional musicians alike can create and perform music.

The mass, motet and cantata are types of vocal music composed for religious occasions, and are usually performed by a group of singers, such as a **choir**.

Mass

A mass is a musical setting of the different parts of the church service known as **Eucharist** or **Communion**. Masses are often sung in Latin, but more modern masses, particularly in the Anglican church, may be in English. A mass usually has five sections:

1   **Kyrie** (Lord have mercy; Christ have mercy)
2   **Gloria** (Glory to God in the highest)
3   **Credo** (I believe in one God)
4   **Sanctus** (Holy, holy, holy) – which also includes **Osanna** (Hosanna) and **Benedictus** (Blessed is he that cometh in the name of the Lord)
5   **Agnus Dei** (Lamb of God)

There may be different versions of this plan depending on the occasion or purpose for which a mass has been composed. A **requiem** is a mass for the dead, with extra sections appropriate for this occasion.

Listening activity

1   The CD has two excerpts of music taken from different masses. The first is the opening of the Credo from Haydn's *Missa in Angustiis*, also known as the 'Nelson' Mass (CD track 9). This is an example of a canon.

The orchestra introduces the main theme of the canon, joined by sopranos and tenors, who start singing the melody in **octaves**. After one bar, the altos and basses start to sing the melody, again in octaves, although their version is written a **fifth** below the original pitch. The two parts shadow each other in this way throughout the excerpt, creating, along with the orchestra, a **polyphonic/contrapuntal** texture.

Now listen to the opening of the Rex tremendae (King of tremendous majesty) from Mozart's Requiem (CD track 10). Like Haydn, Mozart starts with the orchestra. Listen for the 'skipping' **dotted rhythms** in both the orchestral and vocal parts, which are a major feature of the music, and also the variety of different *textures* Mozart uses, starting with a **harmonic/homophonic** texture when the choir first sing the words 'Rex tremendae majestatis', a **polyphonic/contrapuntal** texture when the words are repeated for the second time, and then a section in **octaves** before the music is repeated with new musical material added.

Objectives

You will learn:

about the mass

about the motet

about the cantata

about the oratorio

about the madrigal.

Key terms

Choir: group of singers in which there are a number of singers to each part. A **mixed voice** choir contains both male and female singers, usually **soprano** and **alto** voices (the high and low categories of women's voices) and **tenor** and **bass** (the high and low categories of men's voices) – often abbreviated to SATB. Other choirs might have just women's or just men's voices.

Canon: a particular type of imitation (see page 25).

Motet

The word **motet** is taken from the French word *mots*, meaning 'words'. During the **Renaissance** period (1450–1600) a motet was a sacred (religious) piece, composed for voices. The texture of the music was mainly **polyphonic/contrapuntal** with much use of imitation, where a melodic idea in one voice-part would then be copied, in turn, by each of the other voice-parts. Motets are often performed **a cappella** – by the singers only, without accompanying instruments.

Cantata and oratorio

A **cantata** is usually for one or two solo voices and choir, accompanied by instruments. Cantatas can be **sacred** or **secular**. They are often made up of **recitatives** (where a solo voice sings in a style which resembles half singing, half reciting), **arias** and **choruses**. Recitatives and arias are often paired, the aria following the recitative.

An oratorio is a setting of a religious story. Like a cantata, it has recitatives, arias and choruses, and is accompanied by an orchestra. A commentator – not one of the characters, but a kind of narrator – often sings the recitatives. One of the most famous oratorios is *Messiah* by Handel.

Madrigal

Madrigals are secular songs, sung by a group of solo voices, and are often about life, love and nature. They became popular in Italy during the 16th century, and spread to England when a collection of Italian madrigals was published there in 1588. There was a craze for madrigals in Elizabethan England. English composers caught on to this, and were soon writing madrigals of their own.

Listening activity

3 Compare the recitative 'Behold a virgin shall conceive' with the aria that follows it, 'O thou that tellest good tidings to Zion', from the oratorio *Messiah* by Handel (CD track 12). Note the simple melody and accompaniment in the recitative and the more elaborate vocal melody and instrumental accompaniment of the aria, which begins with a lengthy instrumental introduction.

Listening quiz

Listen to this excerpt taken from the madrigal 'Now is the month of maying' by the English composer Thomas Morley (CD track 13).

1 Which two terms best describe the texture at the opening of this excerpt, on the words 'Now is the month of maying, when merry lads are playing'?

harmonic/homophonic   canonic   octaves   unison   a cappella

2 To what new key has the piece modulated at the end of this phrase, on the word 'playing'?

relative major   relative minor   subdominant   dominant

3 Suggest a possible time signature for this excerpt.

Listening activity

2 Listen to the opening of the motet *O sacrum convivium* (CD track 11) by the Renaissance English composer Thomas Tallis. It has all of the features described left. It is **a cappella**, having no instrumental accompaniment, and uses imitation to create a rich **polyphonic/contrapuntal** texture where the different voice parts weave together their individual melodies.

Key terms

Sacred: based on religious texts.

Secular: based on non-religious texts or stories.

Recitative: a sung recitation. The melody closely follows the rhythm, and rise and fall in pitch of the words. It is used to tell the story. Recitatives are usually accompanied in a simple style, often by plain chords on a harpsichord with a cello playing the bass line.

Aria: literally means 'air', and refers to a lengthy vocal solo (or sometimes a duet), which emphasises the technique of the singer, or reflects on the story or plot.

Chorus: a movement or section of music performed by a choir.

AQA Examiner's tip

Try to recognise the musical features which relate to the five Areas of Study when you listen to excerpts of vocal music.

Activity

Madrigals are music for singers to perform as a fun, social activity. Find the music for some madrigals and try singing them with your class or friends.

3.5 Music for voices: operas and songs

Opera

An opera is a play set to music. Like a play, it is acted and has scenery, costumes and characters, but the words are usually sung throughout to the accompaniment of an orchestra. The first operas were written and performed at the beginning of the 17th century, and have continued to be popular ever since. Like the cantatas and oratorios discussed earlier, operas use **recitatives** to tell the story and move the action on, **arias** to show off a good tune and vocal technique, and **choruses** where the choir can join the action. Opera has always been something special to watch and listen to, often using spectacular stage effects, and sometimes featuring superstar singers. (Female opera stars are sometimes called *divas*.)

Listening activities

1. Listen to the aria 'One fine day' from the opera *Madame Butterfly* by the Italian composer Puccini (CD track 14). The opera is set in Japan at the beginning of the 20th century, and is about a young Japanese girl who falls in love with an older American sailor. 'One fine day' is sung by the heroine, Cio-Cio San (Madame Butterfly), as she imagines her lover, Lieutenant Pinkerton, returning to her. Unfortunately the opera does not have a happy ending! How does the music reflect the emotion and text? Discuss this with someone else, or as a class.

2. Now listen to an excerpt from the duet 'Au fond du temple saint' from Bizet's opera *The Pearl Fishers* (CD track 15). This is one of the most famous and popular of all operatic duets. Two friends are singing about their former rivalry for the love of the same woman, and how, as part of their friendship, they have sworn never to see her again. Why do you think the duet is so popular? In what ways does it suggest friendship and rivalry? Although the words may be in a different language, the music should be able to create the mood.

3. In what way do both pieces show off the skill and technique of the singers? Can you hear places where the singers use vibrato, a trembling effect that is used to produce a warmer, more emotional sound?

Music for solo voice

Solo songs have always been popular. In much folk music, the singer, with no accompaniment, performs the music on his or her own. This is an example of a **single line melody** or **monophonic** texture (see page 25). Or there may be an accompaniment, perhaps a **drone** (see page 19) or some sort of **harmonic** accompaniment.

Strophic and through-composed

In some pieces of vocal music, the same music is used for each verse or section of the text (**strophic** form – see page 40), but in some vocal

Objectives

You will learn:

about opera

about music for solo voice.

Activity

With a friend, or as a class, write down the names of any operas or opera singers you have heard of. Ask other people, in and out of school, to name an opera or opera singer they have heard of. Compare your results with others. Are there any similarities? Why? Find out more about an opera or singer who appears on your list, and try to listen to some performances or recordings.

Key terms

Vibrato: this literally means 'quivering' or 'shaking', and is an effect caused by small, rapid changes to the pitch of a note.

compositions the changing mood or nature of the text determines the structure of the music, so that fresh music will be composed to reflect these changes (**through-composed** – see page 40). Both of these forms can be found in **lieder** (*Lieder* is simply the German word for 'songs', but during the 19th century it became associated with a particular type of song, where the voice and accompaniment are equal in importance).

 Madame Butterfly *by Puccini*

Listening quiz

Listen to the aria 'O ruddier than the cherry' from the opera *Acis and Galatea* by Handel (CD track 18). It is sung by a one-eyed giant called Polypheme. He has just introduced himself in a recitative. This is an example of a **da capo aria** (see page 40 for a description of this form). When the singer goes back to the beginning to repeat section A, it is common practice to introduce some variation. The singer might **improvise**, or add **ornaments** and decorations to the music.

In this aria you can hear examples of a **melisma**. This is where a word that has only one or two syllables (in this case the word 'merry') is sung with a flourish of many different notes.

1   Which word best describes the tonality of this music?

major   minor   modal   pentatonic

2   Suggest a possible time signature for this excerpt.

3   Describe the texture of section B, beginning with the words 'Ripe as the melting cluster'.

4   Name the cadence at the end of the excerpt.

Listening activities

4   Listen to the opening two verses of the lied 'Nähe des Geliebten' ('Nearness of the beloved') by Schubert (CD track 16). In it, the singer is thinking of his beloved.

The mood and nature of the words does not change. In the first verse, for example, the singer imagines his beloved in the sunlight, the sea, in the moonlight or streams. In the other verses he is still thinking of his beloved, but is reminded of her in different ways. Because the nature of the poem does not change, Schubert uses strophic form. After a brief rising piano introduction, which may suggest yearning caused by thoughts of the beloved, the same tune is used for the second (and each successive) verse.

5   Now compare this with 'From far, from eve and morning' by Vaughan Williams (CD track 17). The music for this song is not repeated for different verses. It is through-composed, because the text unfolds a continuous narrative (story).

AQA   Examiner's tip

There are many different kinds of song forms. You will come across others in the section on popular music of the 20th and 21st centuries. Listen carefully to the melody; it will help you to recognise whether a song is strophic (repeated), through-composed (continuous), or has different sections.

Chamber music

Chamber music is intended for performance in a room (or chamber), rather than in a concert hall or large building. It is written for instruments, rather than voices, and is performed by a small group of solo players, with one performer to each part. Most chamber music is written for 2–9 players, although there are some examples composed for larger numbers. The different sizes of groups are named as follows:

- **duet** (two players)
- **trio** (three players)
- **quartet** (four players)
- **quintet** (five players)
- **sextet** (six players)
- **septet** (seven players)
- **octet** (eight players)
- **nonet** (nine players).

Within these descriptions there could be many different combinations of instruments, particularly in works for larger numbers of players. Some of the common combinations are:

- **duet**: piano with one other instrument, e.g. violin, cello, clarinet, flute or horn
- **trio**: **string trio** (violin, viola, cello) or **piano trio** (piano, violin, cello)
- **quartet**: **string quartet** (2 violins, viola, cello) or **piano quartet** (piano, violin, viola, cello)
- **quintet**: **string quintet** (a string quartet plus an extra viola, cello or a double bass), **piano quintet** (usually piano plus string quartet), other types of quintets that have a string quartet with an extra instrument, such as **clarinet quintet** (clarinet plus string quartet), and various types of **wind quintet** (woodwind instruments plus French horn)
- **sextet**: **string sextet** (2 violins, 2 violas, 2 cellos), or **wind sextet** (for example 2 oboes, 2 horns, 2 bassoons, or 2 clarinets, 2 horns, 2 bassoons).

Objectives

You will learn:

what is meant by 'chamber music'

about the different types of chamber music

Did you know ??????

Chamber music became fashionable from around the middle of the 18th century, when it was performed in small rooms (chambers) in the stately homes and palaces of the aristocracy.

Because it involves a small group of solo performers, many composers wrote chamber music that expresses intimate, concentrated ideas. The string quartet, for example, became popular because its performers were like a group of friends having a (musical) conversation or discussion. This is achieved by passing the musical ideas between the instruments, so that each player has a chance to play and develop the musical 'argument'.

Listening activity

1   Listen to an excerpt from the 4th movement of Bartók's String Quartet no. 4 (CD track 19). The instruments are all being played **pizzicato**, rather than the usual **arco**, which means the strings are being plucked, and not played with a bow. In fact, sometimes the strings are plucked so hard that they hit the fingerboard over which they stretch, producing a slapping sound, like a 'twang'. Sometimes an individual instrument plays two or more notes together (or one after the other, very quickly, like strumming a guitar). This is an example of **double-stopping** (see page 33). The harmony is often **chromatic**, producing a harsh, **dissonant** sound. This is a 20th-century work. In what ways is it different from the Beethoven string quartet on track 20?

Listening quiz

Listen to the excerpt from Schubert's 'Trout' Quintet on track 21 of the CD. It is an example of a **theme and variations** (see page 38).

1   Name the five different instruments.

2   What instrument plays the theme at the opening?

3   What is the interval between the first two notes in the opening theme?

   third   fourth   fifth   sixth

4   What is the tonality at the beginning of the excerpt?

5   Describe the texture at the start of this excerpt.

Listening activity

2   Listen to the opening of Beethoven's String Quartet op. 95 in F minor (CD track 20). It begins with all four instruments playing a short melody or motif (a brief musical idea or motto) together, in octaves. After this, concentrate on listening to the overall texture. It is easy to focus on the 1st violin because it is the highest part, but if you listen carefully you will hear the other instruments sharing and developing the opening motif.

AQA Examiner's tip

Listen to different pieces of chamber music. Try to recognise the instruments and which type of chamber group is playing (e.g. string quartet), as well as listening for features and devices described in the Areas of Study. Examples of chamber music are also a good way of becoming familiar with the structure of a **minuet and trio**, and comparing it to a **scherzo and trio** (see page 40). You will find many examples of these, particularly in the string quartets of Haydn and Beethoven (usually the 3rd movement, marked *Menuetto* or *Scherzo*).

A *A string quartet practises*

What is meant by 'sonata'

The word **sonata** means 'sounded' or 'played'. It was originally used to describe music that was written for and performed by instruments, rather than voices. During the classical period (1750 to around 1810), the term sonata was used to describe a composition for one or two instruments (duet) that was in three or four movements. At least one of the movements (often the first) was in **sonata form** (see page 39). The usual plan of a three-movement sonata was:

- first movement – fast
- second movement – slow
- third movement – fast.

In a four-movement sonata, there is usually a **minuet and trio**, or **scherzo and trio** (see page 40) between the slow movement and the last movement.

The solo sonata

This is a sonata written for one instrument. The most popular solo sonatas during the first half of the 18th century were composed for violin or harpsichord. The Italian composer Domenico Scarlatti (1685–1757) wrote more than 500 sonatas for the harpsichord, mostly in one movement and in **binary form**. However, during the second half of the 18th century, the piano replaced the harpsichord as the principal keyboard instrument, and the three- or four-movement **piano sonata** became the most popular form of solo sonata. The piano, unlike the harpsichord, could vary the **dynamic** (volume) of a note by touch. If you press down a key on the piano harder you will produce a louder sound. This does not happen on a harpsichord: the volume stays the same. The word 'piano' is short for 'pianoforte', which combines the Italian words for 'soft' and 'loud', and the name was coined to show off the piano's unique ability to play different dynamics by varying the touch. Through the 18th and 19th centuries developments in materials and design enabled pianos to increased their **compass** (range of notes) and to produce a sustained, richer quality of sound. This was reflected in the increasing technical difficulty and expressive range of music composed for the piano during this period.

Objectives

You will learn:

what is meant by 'sonata'

about different types of sonata.

Activity

1. Find out more about the harpsichord and the way it works. Compare this with a piano and listen to the sound of both instruments. Listen to recordings of music played on original 18th and 19th century pianos (or modern copies), and compare the sound to a modern piano. What are the differences in sound? How does this affect the music?

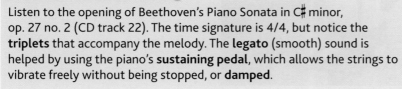

Listening activity

Listen to the opening of Beethoven's Piano Sonata in C♯ minor, op. 27 no. 2 (CD track 22). The time signature is 4/4, but notice the **triplets** that accompany the melody. The **legato** (smooth) sound is helped by using the piano's **sustaining pedal**, which allows the strings to vibrate freely without being stopped, or **damped**.

 A grand piano

Activity

2 A piano can have two or even three pedals. On a piano, experiment by pressing down the pedals and playing the notes to compare the sounds produced. Look inside the piano to see what happens to the mechanism when you press down the different pedals.

The duet sonata

A **duet** is a piece of music written for two players. The most popular type of duet sonatas are those written for a piano in combination with another instrument. The piano's ability to play a wide dynamic range and sustain a sound make it ideal to accompany and interrelate with other instruments. Duet sonatas are often known by the name of the other featured solo instrument (e.g. violin sonata), but the piano is an equal partner.

Listening quiz

Listen to the opening of Beethoven's Violin Sonata no. 5 in F op. 24, 'Spring' (CD track 23). Note the relationship between the violin and piano. First, the violin has the melody with the piano accompanying, then the roles are reversed. Finally both instruments combine to share the musical material. This kind of close relationship is typical of chamber music.

1 Which term best describes the violin melody at the start of the excerpt?

mostly conjunct   mostly disjunct   mostly triadic   mostly arpeggio

2 Which term best describes the piano accompaniment at the start of the excerpt?

scalic   broken chords   pedal   drone

3 Which of these terms best describes the melody?

chromatic   pentatonic   diatonic   modal

AQA Examiner's tip

You can recognise a sonata by listening for a solo instrument, particularly the harpsichord or piano, or a duet including the piano. This kind of question may appear as a multi-choice question, so look at the other possibilities.

3

In this chapter you have learnt:

✔ about the genres and styles which make up this Strand of Learning

✔ what is meant by the 'Western Classical tradition'

✔ about the baroque orchestra

✔ about important baroque composers

✔ about baroque genres and forms such as the suite, solo concerto, concerto grosso and ground bass

✔ what is meant by the term 'classical'

✔ what is meant by the term 'chamber music'

✔ about the different types of chamber music

✔ what is meant by the term 'sonata'

✔ about solo and duet sonatas

✔ key terms relating to the five Areas of Study

✔ how this strand will be tested in the listening examination.

Revision quiz

Try answering the following questions without looking back over the chapter. The answers can be found on p180.

1 Between which dates is the term 'baroque' usually applied to music?

2 What was the most popular keyboard instrument in the baroque period?

3 What is meant by the term 'continuo'?

4 What is the most important section in a baroque orchestra?

5 What name is given to the baroque genre of music which is a collection of different dance pieces?

6 Give the name of one of the most popular dances and describe its main features.

7 What are the names of the solo group and the larger accompanying group in a concerto grosso?

8 Describe what kind of contrasts could be achieved in a solo concerto or concerto grosso.

9 What name is given to a chamber group consisting of five players?

10 What does the word 'sonata' mean?

4 Popular music of the 20th and 21st centuries

Introduction

This chapter will cover:

- Blues
- Popular music of the 1960s, R 'n' B (rhythm and blues), hip-hop
- Rock music
- Music theatre
- Film music

What is meant by the term 'popular music'

This is a term often used to describe any style of music which is not **classical**, or 'serious', or that has been composed with the aim of achieving immediate popularity, appealing to a wide audience which may have little or no musical training. Compare this with the definition of classical music on page 46. In order to catch the listener's ear, popular songs often include the use of catchy melodies, **riffs**, a strong bass line, a memorable structure that is not too long, and a typical and recognisable combination of instruments. Repetition is a major factor in making the music easy to remember. Popular pieces are usually quite short, often lasting less than five minutes.

kerboodle!

4.1 The blues

Blues music started in the southern, slave areas of America during the 19th century, and was a kind of folk music that expressed the feelings and fears of African-Americans, and the conditions in which they lived. Later, blues music spread to the cities, and became associated with the poor, unfortunate and homeless – or, as in many popular music lyrics, unfortunate in love! Blues music is raw, full of emotion, typical of its humble roots. Originally, blues songs were performed by a solo singer, usually accompanied by an instrument that could provide simple harmony, such as a banjo, guitar or piano.

■ 12-bar blues

The 12-bar blues forms the basic structure upon which blues pieces are composed and performed. It is based on a pattern using three different **chords** with a steady four beats to each bar. In a **major scale**, chords built on the first, fourth and fifth notes of the scale (I, IV and V) are all **major** chords. These are often known as the **primary chords**, because between them they include all the notes of the scale. Look at the example below of the primary chords in C major. You can see that between them they contain all of the notes of the scale of C major. This means that they can be used to **harmonise** any tune in the **key** of C major.

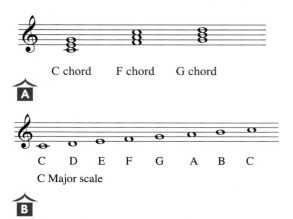

In a 12-bar blues structure, these chords are played in a set order. A typical 12-bar blues chord structure is:

C	/	/	/	C	/	/	/	C	/	/	/	C	/	/	/
F	/	/	/	F	/	/	/	C	/	/	/	C	/	/	/
G	/	/	/	F	/	/	/	C	/	/	/	C	/	/	/

The dashes after each chord indicate that the chord is played four times in each bar to a **crotchet** beat. The 12-bar blues is repeated for each **verse**. Repetition is an important feature of popular music, because it meant that untrained composers and performers could quickly and easily learn the music, and then **improvise** over the basic structure.

Activity

Try playing the 12-bar blues on a guitar or keyboard. Sometimes **seventh chords**, particularly **G⁷** (the notes G B D, plus F) are used (see page 21). Try playing the triad, and then adding the 7th. Listen to the difference.

■ Blue notes

A melodic feature of blues is its use of **blue notes**. These are **chromatic** notes, usually **flats** (lowered by a semitone). In a C blues scale, the blue notes might be:

When added to the melody, these blue notes add a bitter quality, particularly when they clash, or are **dissonant** with the harmony. This adds an expressive quality which stems from the origins of the blues.

■ Rhythm

As we have already learnt, blues music has a steady four-beat rhythm. However, this does not mean every note has to be a crotchet. A characteristic of blues rhythms is the use of syncopation (see page 16), which adds a spiky 'off-beat' feel to the music.

■ Instrumental and vocal techniques

Blues lyrics are expressive and emotional. They tell of hardship and bad luck. To add this expression in the music, singers and instrumentalists often *slide* between a blue note and an ordinary note of the scale (e.g. E♭ to E♮). This produces an effect similar to sighing in human speech. Singers and instrumentalists may also add **vibrato** (see page 33) to add a 'trembling' emotional quality to the sound.

Listening activity

Listen to 'Careless love blues' sung by Bessie Smith (CD track 24) and try to pick out the following features:

- Steady four-beat rhythm (noticeable in the piano chords)
- An instrumental introduction
- A **verse** based on the 12-bar blues
- The use of **vibrato** and **slides** in the vocal and instrumental parts
- Short melodic **phrases** (sung by Bessie Smith) which are repeated after an instrumental link, helping to build up a memorable melody line
- An instrumental link into the second verse, which is the same as the first verse but with slight changes.

a   What changes occur in the second verse? Why do you think they are there? What effect do they have?

b   Identify the two brass instruments used in this piece.

Blues became the inspiration for many other popular music styles, either in their use of structure, chords, melodic features, metre and rhythm, or through performers being inspired by, and basing their music and performance techniques and styles on, blues singers and players.

Did you know ??????

Bessie Smith (1894–1937) was the most popular female blues singer in the 1920s and 1930s. She was tall (over six feet), and had a powerful voice and commanding presence. This helped in the early days of recording, before sensitive microphones became available, when only relatively loud sounds could be recorded.

AQA Examiner's tip

Listen for features such as blue notes and the different chords, including 7th chords, which might be tested in the examination.

Did you know ??????

The 1960s group the Rolling Stones took their name from a song by the blues singer Muddy Waters, and their music is heavily influenced in its style and performance by the blues.

■ Rhythm'n'blues

During the 1960s, pop musicians developed musical styles that had emerged during the 1950s, often creating new and exciting forms of popular music. Two important styles that had a major impact on popular music during the 1960s were **rhythm'n'blues** and **rock'n'roll**. Rhythm'n'blues had developed in the clubs and dance halls of American cities such as Chicago. It mixed the strong vocal style and harmony of **gospel** music with **city-blues** instrumentation, using electric guitars and amplification. Although it was based on the 12-bar blues structure, rhythm'n'blues was often faster, louder and had tighter rhythms.

■ Rock'n'roll

Rock'n'roll was also a mixture, or **fusion**, of two popular music styles: rhythm'n'blues and country & western music. Fast, loud, and using energetic **syncopated** rhythms, rock'n'roll was one of the most important popular music styles to emerge during the 1950s. It became a craze amongst teenagers, not only for its loud driving rhythms, but also for the way its singers and lyrics challenged adult authority. Many of its performers such as Elvis Presley, Chuck Berry and Little Richard became pop legends, and songs like 'Jailhouse rock', 'Blue suede shoes' and 'Tutti frutti' are popular music classics.

Although originally it used a string bass and piano, rock'n'roll helped to establish the typical pop music instrumental combination of lead and rhythm guitars, bass guitar and drum kit.

> **Objectives**
>
> You will learn:
>
> about rhythm'n'blues and rock'n'roll
>
> about gospel and soul music.

A *Elvis Presley*

■ Gospel and soul

Gospel music has its roots in African-American church services, where it developed from religious songs called **spirituals**. Performed by choirs or groups of singers, gospel music combines the harmonic style of European hymn tunes with **call-and-response** patterns (see page 37) and syncopated rhythms from West African music and melodic features of blues music (**blue notes**). Gospel can be very energetic, but its main features are:

- a powerful solo singer, often improvising over a choral background
- the use of **melisma** (see page 55) to extend certain words to make them more important, or repeating a syllable a number of times, with gaps in between (e.g. 'Swee - ee - ee - eet Jesus')
- 'sliding' into a note from a higher or lower pitch
- a fervent emotional quality achieved by sobbing or shouting
- sophisticated vocal arrangements with strong harmonies.

Gospel singing is often accompanied by a keyboard (typically piano or electric organ), drum kit, and bass guitar.

Soul music is a mix of rhythm'n'blues and gospel music. The use of saxophones, brass, electric guitars, drums and amplifiers are an influence of rhythm'n'blues, while the vocal style and the addition of an electric organ come from gospel music. In soul music, the religious words of gospel are replaced by lyrics about human relationships, heartbreak and love, but the vocal style, featuring a powerful solo voice, often backed by slick vocal harmony and featuring solo improvisation and vocal effects to emphasise certain words or phrases, is pure gospel.

Research study

Gospel influences in soul music

Listen to some pieces of soul music written in the 1960s. Try to identify the instruments, and any vocal techniques taken from gospel music. Notice how the backing singers, or **bvox** (short for backing vocals), often 'comment' on a line or phrase the solo vocalist has just sung, often repeating part of it. This is a typical gospel technique, developed from the call-and-response patterns found in spirituals. Try to find some examples of spirituals, such as 'Go down, Moses' and sing them through as a class.

4.3 Popular music of the 1960s: other forms

Pop ballads

Ballads have always been a popular form of song, found quite often in folk music. A ballad is usually a solo song with a fairly slow tempo, a memorable tune, and sometimes a text that is romantic or sentimental. Ballads often tell a story, so the style is usually simple and direct. Many ballads are in **strophic form** (see page 40), with the same music accompanying different verses.

Folk-influenced music

Folk music is a term usually associated with the traditional vocal and instrumental music of a particular country. Its composers are often unknown, and it is music that was originally created and performed by ordinary people. Folk music often provides some sort of social comment, and during the 1960s singers such as Bob Dylan wrote and performed music in a simple folk-style which dealt with issues such as the war in Vietnam, civil rights and the nuclear arms race, which concerned many young people at this time. Bob Dylan's music is mostly original rather than traditional; however, it develops a tradition of social protest in American folk music that dates back to the economic depression of the 1930s.

A A folk band

There was a renewed interest in this kind of music amongst students in American and, later, British universities in the 1960s. It was these students who formed protest movements, aimed at changing the issues Bob Dylan was singing about in his music. At first, Dylan performed his music in a simple, traditional way, with an accompaniment of acoustic guitar and harmonica. However, in 1965 he shocked the audience at the Newport Folk Festival when he used an amplified electric guitar and was accompanied by a rock band. To many he had abandoned his traditional folk roots, selling out to a more commercial style. To others he had started a new style of music – folk-rock.

Listening activity

2 Listen to the recording of Bob Dylan singing 'Blowin' in the wind'. The song has a straightforward melody and a simple chordal accompaniment on the acoustic guitar. After a short guitar **introduction**, 'Blowin' in the wind' has a repeated **verse-chorus** structure typical of many popular songs. In between each verse there is a short instrumental **link**, played by the guitar and harmonica. After the final chorus, the instrumental link is played as a **coda**.

▮ Popular song form

Popular song form is usually 32 bars long. The 32 bars are divided into four sections, each of eight bars. The first two sections and the last section all use the same melody. The third section, however, has a different melody, and may be in a different key, so that the overall plan is:

A   A   B   A

The B section is sometimes called a 'middle 8' referring to its length in bars, and its relative position in the plan. Many pop songs written during the 1960s are based on popular song form.

B *Bob Dylan*

Activity

Compose and perform your own piece in popular song form. Use the notes of the scale of C major. Make sure that each section is 8 bars long, and that you follow the popular song form plan. For your B section try composing a melody in a different key, say F major, and see if you can find a note that links back successfully into the final A section.

Although the origins and development of popular music styles had taken place in America, during the 1960s British groups began to play a major part in creating a new and exciting popular music scene. In fact, some British groups, such as the Beatles, became so popular both in Britain and America that they directly influenced American popular music.

The Beatles

The Beatles had their first big chart success early in 1963 with 'Please please me'; by 1964, a string of number one hit singles had made the four band members – John Lennon, Paul McCartney, Ringo Starr and George Harrison – famous in both Britain and America. At the start of their first American tour a crowd of 3,000 screaming fans greeted them at New York's John F. Kennedy airport, and 'Beatlemania' followed the band wherever they went. Although their music sounded new and fresh, the Beatles had in fact learned their trade in the clubs of Hamburg and elsewhere in Europe, and their music drew on a wide range of styles, including rhythm'n'blues, rock'n'roll and country & western. In 1967 they met the Maharishi Mahesh Yogi in London, and thereafter spent some time in India, where they became influenced by Indian classical music (incorporating the sitar, for example, into their music). After 1967 the Beatles became more experimental, making use of unusual instrumental combinations and effects, and new and different structures.

Objectives

You will learn:

about British popular music in the 1960s

about some of the important musicians of this period.

Did you know ??????

Ironically, the noise created by screaming fans was often more powerful than the amplifiers the Beatles used to play their music, with the result that they could be seen, but not heard in live concerts!

Research study 🔍

1 **The Beatles**

Find out more about the Beatles and the different popular music styles that influenced their music. Listen to and compare early songs like 'She loves you' and albums like *With the Beatles* with later songs such as 'Strawberry Fields forever' and the album *Sergeant Pepper's Lonely Hearts Club Band*. In what ways does the music change between these two periods?

The Rolling Stones

The Rolling Stones – Mick Jagger, Keith Richards, Brian Jones, Bill Wyman and Charlie Watts – were the opposite of the Beatles. Where the Beatles wore smart collarless jackets and were charming and personable, the Rolling Stones were scruffy, casual, and had a provocative manner that enraged adults. Their music was raw and distinctive, inspired by rhythm'n'blues, and characterised by **distorted** guitar sounds and a harsh, thick instrumental **mix**.

A *The Rolling Stones*

The Who

The Who were formed in 1964, with an original line-up of guitarist Pete Townshend, vocalist Roger Daltry, John Entwistle on bass, and drummer Keith Moon. Their music was characterised by frenzied, wild performances that often ended with Townshend smashing his guitar on stage. Townshend used **feedback** and **power chords** to add power and aggression to the music. The Who's music was greatly admired by the **Mods**, a popular youth culture of the period.

> **Key terms**
>
> **Feedback**: a loud whining sound created by over-amplifying the guitar.
>
> **Power chord**: an open chord, containing just the root and fifth of a chord.

Research study

2   The Mods

Find out more about the Mods and the Who, and how their music and that of the Beatles and Rolling Stones reflected social attitudes in Britain during the 1960s.

Listening quiz

Listen to 'I can't get no Satisfaction' by the Rolling Stones.

1   Describe the effect or technique used by the guitars in this excerpt.

2   What effect does this have on the music?

3   What term best describes the short, repeated guitar melody heard at the beginning of the music?
scalic   sequence   riff   triadic

4   What term best describes the rhythm of this guitar melody?
irregular   rubato   polyrhythmic   syncopated

5   Which of the following rhythms matches the rhythm of the opening guitar melody?

a

b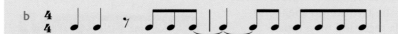

c

d

4.5 Rock music

What is meant by rock music

Rock music developed out of rock'n'roll. It is a **genre** of popular music which often has an instrumental group of electric lead guitar, bass guitar, drum kit and sometimes a keyboard, often an electronic keyboard or synthesiser. There is an emphasis on the lead guitar and a strong **back beat** – beats 2 and 4 in 4/4 metre:

Rock music is often extremely loud and exciting, displaying **virtuoso** performances (brilliant technique and showmanship). Sometimes it expresses anger and frustration.

There are many different types of rock music, the main categories being:

- psychedelic rock
- progressive rock
- hard rock
- punk rock.

Psychedelic rock

This style of rock music tries to recreate the mind-altering experience of drugs. It emerged during the 1960s when it was felt that the taking of certain drugs, such as LSD, that caused hallucinations and distorted time and sensation could take the mind to a higher plane of experience and understanding. Of course, this was not a permanent state, and for many it was a disaster, resulting in addiction and depression, sometimes death. Psychedelic rock is characterised by strange, weird lyrics, the use of unusual and exotic instruments, such as the *sitar* and *tabla*, extended instrumental solos and the use of technological effects such as **panning** (moving sound between the two stereo speakers), **reverb** (see page 32) and reversing sounds recorded on a tape.

Progressive rock

Progressive rock emerged during the late 1960s. It extended the normal 3–5 minutes of popular music forms into pieces lasting up to 15 minutes or more. In this sense it tried to copy classical music and jazz, where the development of musical ideas takes much more time. Progressive rock pieces often involve lengthy instrumental solos, copying the improvised solos in jazz, and slow-moving chord patterns. Progressive rock groups often unified their ideas in **concept albums**, which have an underlying theme, or tell an epic story.

Objectives

You will learn:

about rock music

about psychedelic rock

about progressive rock

about hard rock

about punk rock.

Activity

Research and listen to some examples of psychedelic rock and try to identify the different technological effects. What effect do they have on the music?

Listening activity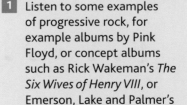

1 Listen to some examples of progressive rock, for example albums by Pink Floyd, or concept albums such as Rick Wakeman's *The Six Wives of Henry VIII*, or Emerson, Lake and Palmer's pop version of Mussorgsky's *Pictures at an Exhibition*. What influences from classical music or jazz can you identify in these pieces?

Hard rock

Hard rock, or heavy rock, has an emphasis on the solo guitar. It plays **riffs**, virtuoso **solos** using many different techniques that help the speed of playing, and **fills** (see page 41). Typical instrumentation comprises solo guitar, bass guitar, drum kit, keyboards (usually electronic organ or synthesiser) and vocalist. Hard rock often uses a range of tonalities, including **modal** scales (see page 23).

Punk rock

Punk rock developed during the mid-1970s, and was a reaction against the commercial and intellectual developments of rock music. In the eyes of punk musicians, rock music had abandoned its roots and become too complicated. Rock music was the music of the 'superstar' performer – comfortable and elite. Punk rock demanded a return to the raw side of rock music – the simple chords and structures of rock'n'roll, and the rebellious attitudes found in its singers and audiences.

Punk music often contains a limited number of chords, played at a fast tempo, and **distorted**. The melody is a mixture of shouted rants, and the structure is often simple and repetitive, with an unvarying, powerful rhythm. The lyrics are provocative and anti-establishment, even **anarchic**.

Listening activity

2 Listen to 'Child in Time' by Deep Purple. The opening organ riff is modal, so listen for the characteristic tone between the leading note and tonic – in this case the first three notes, which are repeated to form the riff.

Research study

Punk rock

Find out more about punk rock, its fashions, groups and style. In what ways did punk rock return to the original ideals of rock music?

 Punk rockers

Listening quiz

1 Listen to 'On the run' from Pink Floyd's album *Dark Side of the Moon*

a What term best describes the rhythm and melody heard in this excerpt?
broken chords   chromatic   sequence   ostinato

b What electronic keyboard instrument can be heard in this excerpt?

c What effect do the electronic effects have on the music?

4.6 Hip-hop and music theatre

Hip-hop

Hip-hop is a genre of music which emerged in New York during the 1970s when **DJs** (disc jockeys) began to **loop** percussion breaks taken from **funk** or rock songs to create a powerful rhythmic 'beat' for their audiences to dance to. In hip-hop terms, the beat is everything but the vocals. It is often built up in layers, including the basic audio loop of a drum track or midi drum patterns, a bass line, supporting orchestration such as a synthesiser and a variety of sound samples. The shortest beats are usually 8 bars long, but can be looped to produce beats of any length.

One feature of the music is the 'break', where the drum (or electronic/computer-generated sound) plays a short solo.

This was later accompanied by **rapping**, where the performer, often the DJ, speaks rhythmically and in rhyme to the beat.

Loops were originally created on tape, but developments in technology have enabled musicians to create and modify loops digitally, even in live performance, while also being able to add other electronic effects by using **samplers** and **synthesisers**. A sampler is a device that stores recordings of many different sounds (samples) as digital information, which can then be played and modified in many different ways.

Hip-hop musicians have experimented by using different genres of music to create new and exciting beats, and to develop different styles of hip-hop. Rhythm'n'Bass is one of those styles, where there is an emphasis on projecting a strong bass line in the music.

Key terms

Loop: a sample of sound, or a short section of recorded music, that is repeated continuously.

Funk: a style of music developed from soul, rhythm'n'blues and jazz. It is raw and exciting, with an emphasis on the bass line and rhythm. In funk, the bass guitar creates a distinctive, percussive effect caused by slapping the strings. Strong bass and drum rhythms combine with the other instruments to give a strong **polyrhythmic** feel to the music.

Listening quiz

1 Listen to 'Good Life' by Kanye West. Notice how the beat is built up using different sound loops, including a synthesiser and electronic drum and rhythm effects. Over this there is rapping with the voices electronically changed in places.

  a What term best describes the synthesiser melody heard at the start of the piece?

  b What term best describes the tonality of this song?

   major   minor   modal   pentatonic

Research study

Hip-hop culture

Hip-hop is a whole culture, involving dancing, fashions, art and a varied music scene. Find out more about hip-hop either through magazine articles or by using the internet.

■ Music theatre

Music theatre works are generally referred to as **musicals**. Like opera, a musical is a play which uses music to express emotion. Like a play, it has characters, scenery and costumes and tells a story. However, like opera it makes use of **solo songs**, duets, **ensembles** and **choruses** to express the emotion of the words, and is accompanied by instruments, usually an orchestra. There are some differences between musicals and opera. Spoken dialogue is used more frequently in musicals than in opera, as well as dancing. Musicals are often influenced by popular music styles such as rock, blues or jazz, and use electric guitars, keyboards and amplifiers to boost the volume of the singers and instruments. An opera is usually sung in the language in which it was composed, by professionally trained singers. However, a musical is more often sung in the language of its audience, and the singers are actors first, rather than professionally trained singers, which is one reason why amateur performances of musicals are so common.

Music theatre is big business. Theatres in major cities, such as London and New York, offer a wide choice of musicals, ranging from established classics such as *The Phantom of the Opera* (Andrew Lloyd Webber) and *Les Misérables* (Claude-Michel Schönberg) to productions of brand new musicals.

> **Activity**
>
> Ask people you know to tell you about any musicals they have been to see, and what they enjoyed about them. Perhaps your school is producing or has produced a musical. Find out more about who wrote it and what popular style of music it is based on. Perhaps you could interview one of the singers about their role and the music they sang.

Listening quiz

2 Listen to 'Bring him home' from the musical *Les Misérables*. This song is sung by the character Valjean. Although it is sung by a **tenor** voice, much of the music is written higher than the singer's vocal range, so that he has to sing **falsetto** (see page 33).

a   What effect does this have on the music?

b   Why do you think the vocal part has been written this way?

c   Which plan best represents the structure of this excerpt?

ABA   ABC   ABB   AAB

d   What is the tonality of this excerpt?

e   What is the interval between the first two notes sung by Valjean?
fourth   fifth   sixth   octave

A Les Misérables

Film music

Music is often used to accompany a scene in a film. In the early 20th century, when films had no sound (silent movies) it was common to find a pianist **improvising** music which fitted what was happening on the screen. This is the power of music – to be able to create a mood or feeling, an emotional response in the listener. This is very useful in films, where it can be used to enhance the mood or drama of a particular scene, or help to create the right mood for a scene that is about to happen. Like opera, which often starts with an **overture** (an 'opening' piece of instrumental music composed as an introduction), films often begin with an opening piece of music set against the titles, to help capture the audience's attention and set the right mood.

Conventions and leitmotifs

Like most music composed for a specific occasion or event, film music often makes use of **conventions**. These are musical devices and features that listeners associate with something *extra-musical* (outside of the music) and can be used by composers to create a particular **context** in the music. For example, music for Western films often includes a harmonica, train-whistle sounds, or 'galloping' rhythms, because these instruments or musical devices are associated with the 'Wild West', and using them helps the composer to create the right mood and context.

> **Activity**
>
> Working on your own, in pairs or as a group, choose a scene from a film and compose music to match the mood and action. Plan and discuss your piece, and then listen to each group's compositions. Choose one you particularly like and say why it was successful.

A **leitmotif** (originally German, meaning leading-motive) is a memorable and distinctive theme or musical idea that is used throughout a piece to represent a person, object, idea or emotion. In short, it is a musical 'tag'. Leitmotifs are very useful in film music: they help the audience to establish a link with a character or object in a film, and can even be played when the character or object is not actually on-screen, suggesting some connection between what is happening and the character. A leitmotif can be changed in some way to create a different mood or situation affecting the character or object. This device is also used in opera, in much the same way.

> **Objectives**
>
> You will learn:
>
> about film music
>
> about conventions used in film music
>
> about leitmotifs.

> **Key terms**
>
> **Context**: context in music includes taking into account the occasion, purpose and place the music was composed for, the time (age) in which was written, and the time and place in which it was performed.

> **AQA Examiner's tip**
>
> In the listening examination you may be asked to recognise any features from the Areas of Study, but there are likely to be questions that relate to recognising instruments and techniques and texture.

A *Advertisement for the film Jaws*

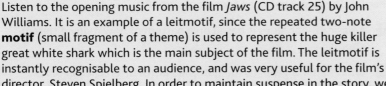

Listen to the opening music from the film *Jaws* (CD track 25) by John Williams. It is an example of a leitmotif, since the repeated two-note **motif** (small fragment of a theme) is used to represent the huge killer great white shark which is the main subject of the film. The leitmotif is instantly recognisable to an audience, and was very useful for the film's director, Steven Spielberg. In order to maintain suspense in the story, we do not actually see the shark itself until well into the film, by which time it has disposed of several people. However, the audience knows when the shark is going to attack, or is around, because they hear its leitmotif. This enables Spielberg to save the big moment when the shark's huge size is revealed to the audience until much later.

The leitmotif itself also conveys much of the shark's 'character'. The two notes are simple and direct (an unsophisticated hunting, eating machine), they are a **semitone** apart (threatening), and often played at a low pitch (indicating size and depth). The two-note motif gets faster and louder (suggesting an attack).

1 Which term best describes the harmony of this excerpt?

2 Which term best describes the melodic shape played by the French horn and then repeated by the woodwind near the start of the excerpt?
   conjunct   disjunct   scalic

3 Name the plucked string instrument heard towards the end of the excerpt.

4 Which two of the following can you hear in the excerpt?
   trill   ostinato   canon   syncopation   drum fill

5 Name one percussion instrument you can hear in the excerpt.

4

In this chapter you have learnt:

✔ about the genres and styles which make up this Strand of Learning

✔ what is meant by the term 'popular music'

✔ about the blues

✔ about different genres and groups in popular music of the 1960s

✔ about rock music

✔ about hip-hop

✔ about music theatre

✔ about film music

✔ key terms relating to the five Areas of Study

✔ how the strand 'popular music of the 20th and 21st centuries' will be tested in the listening examination.

Revision quiz

Try answering the following questions without looking back over the chapter. The answers can be found on page 180.

1 A basic 12-bar blues is based on a pattern of how many different chords?

2 What name is given to the flattened notes often used in blues melodies?

3 What name is sometimes given to the backing singers found in soul music, for example?

4 What form are most ballads written in?

5 What is the plan of popular song form?

6 What is meant by a **back beat**?

7 What are **power chords**?

8 What is a **leitmotif**?

9 What is a **loop**?

10 What is a **synthesiser**?

Objectives

In this chapter you will learn:

what is meant by the term 'world music'

about the specific types and genres of music which make up this Strand of Learning

how the examination questions will relate to this strand.

Key terms

Fusion: can also refer to the blending of other musical styles, such as jazz and rock.

This chapter will cover:

- Music of the Caribbean
- Music of Africa
- Music of India

What is meant by the term 'world music'

World music is a term often used to describe musical traditions, styles and genres that are non-Western: that is, from outside of Europe and the United States. This includes the traditional folk music and song of a particular region or culture, and non-Western classical and popular music. Some forms and genres of world music have been influenced by Western music, especially popular music styles, instruments and rhythms, which have been combined with non-Western folk and classical traditions to produce a new and unique blend. This combination of Western and non-Western musical styles is called **fusion**. This chapter will focus on some of the musical traditions and genres from the Caribbean, Africa and India, and how traditional elements have been blended with those of Western popular music.

Starter activity

Find out more about the Caribbean, Africa and India. Locate them on a map. What islands, countries or regions make up these areas? Try to find out more about their cultures and history.

 The Caribbean

The Caribbean is a group of some 7,000 islands, islets and reefs located between the United States and South America, and divided into a number of separate countries. Each country has its own particular musical styles and genres, but some styles are shared and can be found all over the Caribbean.

Activity

1 Caribbean music has its roots in other musical traditions, particularly those of Africa and Europe. Find out why it is influenced by music from these countries.

Calypso

This is a style of music that originated in Trinidad and Tobago at the start of the 20th century and spread to other Caribbean islands. It is a form of solo song that combines story-telling with memorable tunes and rhythms. Calypso has always been associated with some form of social comment, and is an important feature of **carnival**. Calypso is often performed by the singer accompanied by a guitar, although there can be a larger backing group which might include brass, saxophones, drums and electric guitars.

Listening activity

1 Stars of calypso music include Lord Kitchener and Mighty Sparrow. Listen to examples of calypso music by them or other calypso performers. What do the lyrics tell you? Why is calypso so popular?

Steelbands

After the Second World War, the oil drums left by the Americans on the island of Trinidad were converted into pitched musical drums. Each steel drum, or *pan*, can produce several different notes, and there are different sizes of pan, so that steelbands can play a wide range of notes, like a choir. A steel pan does not *sustain*, so each note is struck repeatedly to produce a characteristic 'shimmering' sound.

Listening activity

2 Try to listen to some live steelband music. Carnivals take place throughout the country, so look out for one near you. Perhaps your school, or a school near you, has its own steelband. Try to listen to it, and talk to some of the players about the special kinds of technique they use, and the roles of the different pans.

Salsa

Salsa means *sauce* in Spanish, and is a type of dance-music associated with Cuba. It developed in the 1960s from a mixture of two traditional dances (the *son* and the *rumba*) with other kinds of American music, such as jazz. Salsa traditionally uses a 4/4 time signature, and is based on a repeated rhythm called *clave*, around which musicians play repeated rhythmic accompaniments. The clave rhythm is central to all salsa, whether it is performed on the claves or by another instrument. The most common clave rhythm is the *son clave*, which is eight beats long and can be played in a 2-3, or 3-2 style.

2 - 3 clave rhythm

3 - 2 clave rhythm

Listening activity

Listen to CD track 26. Notice the use of jazz features, such as the brass, combined with vibrant salsa rhythms and textures.

Reggae

Reggae developed in Jamaica at the end of the 1960s, emerging from two forms of Jamaican popular music, *ska* and *rock steady*. Ska combined elements of **mento**, jazz and rhythm'n'blues to create a lively musical style, which had an emphasis on the second and fourth beats of the bar. During the mid-1960s, the beat of ska was slowed down to produce rock steady, a more vocal style of music which used **riffs**, a limited number of chords, and a strong bass line. Like ska and rock steady, reggae makes use of syncopated rhythms and a characteristic **backbeat** (emphasis on beats 2 and 4). Another important characteristic of reggae is the solid bass line, which features catchy melodic riffs played by the electric bass guitar.

Listening quiz

Listen to 'One love' by Bob Marley. Notice the 'chopped' guitar chords on beats 2 and 4 and the distinctive bass riff.

1 Which **two** words best describe the bass line?
   dotted   rhythms   triplets   syncopation   hemiola   arpeggio

2 Name the instrument playing the melody at the beginning of the song.

3 After the solo drum beats at the start of the song, how many bars of instrumental music are played before the voice enters?

4 What type of voices accompany the solo singer in this piece?
   male   female   mixed voices   children's voices

5 After the instrumental introduction, which term best describes the structure of the song?
   through-composed   rondo   chorus/verse   call and response

Music in Africa

Africa is a vast continent with many different regions and nations, each with its own traditions and identity. Music plays an important part in African society. It has religious, ritual and ceremonial functions, as well as being used at social gatherings. African music has its roots in legends, mythology and folklore, and is used to communicate feelings and emotions that express the way the society in which it is produced views the world. Music is often combined with dance; in fact, in some African languages they are both described by one word. Traditional African music is an **oral tradition**, and was never written down. Despite Africa's diverse and different cultures, there are some musical features, such as rhythm patterns, structures, textures and the use of improvisation, that unite the music of various groups and areas.

African choral music

There is a close connection between speech and singing. Many African languages are **tonal languages**, which means that the pitch level at which a word is spoken often determines its meaning. This affects the way melodic and rhythmic patterns in vocal music are created; the unique pitches and *intonation* (tuning) of African music make it difficult to relate to Western notation. Most African melodies are based on four, five, six or seven-note scales. African vocal melodies are usually short and simple, often being extended by repetition and improvisation.

A common way of structuring a choral piece is by using **call and response**. The solo singer starts with a melody, and this is responded to (answered) by the other singers. During a performance it is common for different melodies to be improvised at the same time, producing a rich **polyphonic/contrapuntal** texture. At other times, a **harmonic/ homophonic** texture may be used. In African music this is often created by singing in thirds, fourths or fifths. Unison and **parallel** octave textures are also common.

Objectives

You will learn:

about music in Africa

about African choral music

about popular music in Africa.

Key terms

Parallel motion: two voices moving up or down in pitch, but always keeping the same interval (pitch-distance) between the two notes. The most common examples of this are parallel octaves and parallel fifths.

Activity

See if you can find some songs from Africa in your school's music department. Some of them may be in harmony, so try singing them as a group. Try composing and performing your own call and response song, making up your own words about some aspect of school life.

■ Popular music

African music has been a major influence on the development of popular music, contributing rhythms, structures, melodic features and the use of improvisation to such styles as blues and jazz brought over to America by slaves. More recently, African music has once again been the focus of American popular musicians, contributing its unique vocal and instrumental styles to such albums as Paul Simon's *Graceland*.

Listening activity

Listen to 'Uma Ilanga Liyo' by the Soweto Gospel Choir (CD track 27). What features of traditional African music do you hear, and how has the piece been influenced by other popular music styles?

A *The Nelson Mandela Metropolitan Choir*

Music of Africa: drumming and instrumental music

■ African drumming

The drum is an important musical instrument in African culture. Drums have been used as a means of communication for hundreds of years, and there are many different varieties found throughout the different regions: for example, the *tama* talking drums, *bougarabou* and *djembe* in West Africa. The *djembe* is a single-headed drum which comes in a range of sizes in order to produce different pitch ranges.

Drum music may be performed by a solo instrument or in ensembles. Like vocal music, drum and instrumental music is not notated, so in a drum ensemble the performance is directed by a **master drummer**, who stands in the middle of a circle of drummers. The master drummer often starts a piece by *vocalising* – making sounds with the voice – and then plays a short rhythmic solo to set the **tempo** and mood. This is a cue to the other performers, who respond by copying the rhythm or by answering it with a different rhythm. This is another example of the call and response form. The drummers then add improvised rhythms to a rhythmic cycle.

Activity

With a group of friends or in class, form a circle. If you have a selection of drums, use them, otherwise other percussion instruments will do. (You could have a go at making a home-made drum and bringing it into class.) Choose one person to be the master drummer. The chosen person stands in the middle.

■ The master drummer shouts an opening cue, then plays this cycle:

1	2	3	4	5	6	7	8
x		x	x	x		x	x

■ The other drummers then answer by repeating the cycle continuously.

■ From time to time the master drummer calls out to a member of the group to improvise.

■ More members of the group are asked to improvise at the same time.

■ The master drummer then signals the end of the performance.

Take turns to be the master drummer. Try to create cross rhythms and a polyrhythmic texture. Can you invent creative ways of improvising? Try adding syncopation or accents, or playing the cycle backwards (*retrograde*), or starting on a different number in the cycle (*phasing*).

Objectives

You will learn:

about African drumming

about some African instruments.

A *Tama*

Remember

The drummers often cut across the rhythm, using accents (stressed notes) in different places and on different parts of the beat, producing exciting cross-rhythms. The combination of two contrasting rhythms is called a bi-rhythm. When a number of different rhythms are combined the texture is polyrhythmic.

Did you know ??????

The master drummer can develop the performance by cueing in a new section, often a different **rhythmic cycle**, so that a performance becomes a succession of different, often contrasting, sections. Some sections may include solo improvisations, which allow performers to show off their individual skills.

Key terms

Rhythmic cycle: a rhythm that is continuously repeated. The repeats may be varied in some way.

◼ African instruments

There is a wide variety of African instruments, which are chosen for a particular song or instrumental performance depending on the suitability of their **timbre**. There are many kinds of percussion, wind and string instruments, including different kinds of harp which often have complicated tuning systems. As in African drumming, instrumental music makes use of repetition and ostinato, cyclic structures, improvisation, polyrhythmic and polyphonic/contrapuntal textures.

Xylophone

The xylophone is used in almost all of Africa, but there are different types, depending upon the area. The wooden bars are set on a frame that has gourds (hollow dried shells of fruit) underneath them to help amplify the sound.

Kosika

The *kosika* is a percussion instrument which consists of two small gourds or seed pods filled with beans and connected by a string. One gourd is held in the hand and the other is swung from side to side as you shake your hand. The kosika has two sounds: a 'shake' created by the beans, and a 'clack' when the two gourds or seed pods hit each other.

Kora

A *kora* is built from a large calabash gourd cut in half and covered with cow skin to make a resonator. It has a notched bridge like a lute or guitar. The sound of a kora resembles a harp. The player uses the thumb and index fingers of both hands to pluck the strings, while the remaining fingers hold the instrument. Traditional koras have 21 strings: 11 played by the left hand and 10 by the right. Modern koras often have additional bass strings. Strings were traditionally made from thin strips of hide, but now most strings are made from harp strings or nylon fishing line. A kora player can retune the instrument into one of four seven-note scales by moving leather tuning rings up and down the neck.

B *Xylophone*

C *Kosika*

D *Kora*

AQA Examiner's tip

African music has a variety of rhythmic devices, such as syncopation, cross-rhythms and polyrhythms which could be tested in the listening examination, along with structures like call and response and cyclic forms.

5.4 | Music of India: background and instruments

The music of India

The history of Indian music stretches back over two thousand years. It is one of the oldest musical traditions in the world, and is fundamentally associated with religious and cultural expression. There are two main traditions: the **Hindustani** tradition of northern India and the **Carnatic** tradition of southern India. Indian music is not notated, but is taught from master to pupil by listening and playing. Indian classical music can often be very complex, but there are three common elements:

- **Melody**. This is usually improvised from a type of scale, called a *rag*. The melody might be sung or played on an instrument.
- **Drone**. Indian classical music focuses on the development of **melody**; therefore accompaniments are usually simple. The drone is an accompaniment using only two notes, a fifth apart.
- **Rhythm**. Known as the *tala*, it is organised into repeating **cycles**.

Indian instruments

Apart from the human voice, some of the common instruments found in Indian classical music are:

- the sitar
- the sarangi
- the tabla
- the bansuri
- the shenhai.

The sitar

This is a plucked string instrument. It has seven metal strings, of which two are used to play the drone. Below these are a number of loose strings which vibrate when the strings above them are plucked with a wire plectrum. This produces the characteristic 'twangy' sound that makes the sitar one of the most recognisable Indian instruments.

The sarangi

Smaller than the sitar, with a softer sound, making it ideal as an accompaniment to the voice, the sarangi uses a bow to produce its notes.

The tabla

This is a set of two different sized drums played with both hands. They play the **tala**, or rhythm cycle.

The bansuri and shenhai

These produce sounds similar to the flute and oboe, but do not have the metal keys used by their western counterparts to play the lower notes. The player covers a series of holes with his or her fingers, similarly to the way the recorder is played.

A *Sitar*

B *Sarangi*

C *Tabla*

D *Shenhai*

E *Bansuri*

Music of India: classical and popular styles

Rag

A *rag* (pronounced with a long 'a')is the basic melody which forms the basis for melodic improvisation. It is similar to a Western scale in that it ascends (goes up) and descends (goes down). However, unlike a Western scale each rag is individual, so that the pitches of the notes may vary not only between different rags, but also in the ascending and descending forms. There are also varying numbers of notes in different rags. This is because, unlike a Western scale, each rag has a unique mood, which is associated with a different occasion, season, purpose and emotion. There are over 200 different rags! In a performance the rag is used as the basis for improvisation. Here is an example of a rag called 'rag Marwa', which is an evening rag:

Tala

The tala is a rhythm pattern that forms the basis for a set of repeating rhythmic **cycles**. The tala is usually played by the tabla drums. There are different talas, but the most common tala used in the music of northern India is *tintal* (or *teental*). Tintal is a symmetrical rhythmic pattern made up of four individual, main beats, repeated four times (4 + 4 + 4 + 4). Each individual beat is called a **matras**, and the first beat of the cycle is called a **sam**. During the tala cycle, rhythms are improvised by both the tabla player and the instrumentalist or singer, but must start and end on the first beat of the cycle (the sam). These improvised rhythms, or **bols**, contrast with the main beat of the cycle, often using accents or syncopation, and are similar to the improvisations in jazz or rock music, where each performer tries to outdo the previous improvisation while still keeping within the cycle of beats.

Objectives

You will learn:

about rag and tala

about raga performance

about bhangra.

Activity

1. Play through the rag Marwa at your own rhythm. Experiment with trying to achieve the right 'evening' quality in your performance. Extend the rag by improvising.

Key terms

Cycle: (here) a rhythm, melody or harmony that is continuously repeated. Its repeats may be varied in some way.

Matras: the individual beats in the rhythmic cycle.

Sam: the first beat of the rhythmic cycle.

Bols: improvised rhythms which contrast with the main beat.

Activity

2. Working in a group of three or four, try improvising over this *tintal* tala. Choose different percussion instruments. One player plays the matras (individual beats) at the beginning and then repeats them for each cycle (shown in the grid below). The other players improvise using accents and syncopation (bols), each in turn – but always starting and finishing on the first beat of the cycle (sam). See who can create the most interesting improvisation – but remember to start, and end, on the sam.

1	2	3	4	5	6	7	8	9	10	11	12	13	14	15	16
sam	x	x	x	x	x	x	x	x	x	x	x	x	x	x	x

Raga

A raga performance contains all three of the elements used in Indian classical music: melody (based on a rag), the drone, and the tala rhythm played by the tabla drums. There is usually a defined structure for a raga performance, with different sections. The first section, called **alap**, starts with a slow exploration of the notes of the rag. It is in *free time*, often to the accompaniment of a drone. The final section, called **gat**, contains the rhythmic tala cycle introduced on the tabla, solos, and improvisation. There are often other sections in between the alap and gat, and, since ragas are improvised, they can last for several hours!

Bhangra

Bhangra originated in the Punjab district of India and Pakistan, and is traditionally a kind of folk song/dance performed during harvest. It is now associated with a fusion between Western popular music styles and features of Indian classical music. Bhangra is characterised by the use of Indian instruments such as the *dhol* (a type of drum), repetitive rhythms, and the Punjabi language (with typical shouts of 'hoi'), mixed with Western instruments such as the synthesiser.

B A bangra group

> ### Key terms
>
> **Alap**: the opening section of a raga. Improvised and in free-rhythm.
>
> **Gat**: the final section of a raga. Contains a 'tune' with improvisation and tala.

> ### Listening activity
>
> Listen to an excerpt from a performance of Raga Bhim Palasi, played on the bansuri (CD track 29). At first you hear the alap section. Notice the improvisatory feel as the bansuri explores the various notes of the rag to the accompaniment of a drone, and the lack of pulse, creating a sense of free rhythm. At the end of the alap, the tabla drums enter playing the tala rhythm, using Rupak tal (a 7-beat cycle).

> ### AQA *Examiner's tip*
>
> Try to identify particular instruments, rhythms and the use of improvisation in Indian music. These may be tested in the listening examination.

Listening quiz

Listen to an excerpt from 'Bhangra Fever' by MIDIval Punditz (CD track 30).

1. Name two features of the music which are influenced by traditional Indian music.

2. List two features which show the use of music technology in this excerpt.

3. What is the time signature of this excerpt?

4. Which term best describes the melody?
   whole tone   triadic   ostinato   sequence

5. On which beats of the bar do you hear the shouts 'hoi' or 'hi'?

5

In this chapter you have learnt:

✔ about the genres and styles which make up this Strand of Learning

✔ about music of the Caribbean

✔ about African music

✔ about Indian music

✔ about the different styles and genres which help make up these traditions

✔ key terms relating to the five Areas of Study

✔ how the World music strand will be tested in the listening examination.

Revision quiz

Try answering the following questions without looking back over the chapter. The answers can be found on page 180.

1 Name the two Cuban dances which influenced salsa.

2 What name is given to the central rhythm of salsa music?

3 What beats are emphasised in reggae?

4 Which instrument plays these beats?

5 Name one feature of that instrument's technique in reggae.

6 What is call and response?

7 What is a polyrhythmic texture?

8 What are cross-rhythms?

9 What name is given to the melody that forms the basis for improvisation in Indian music?

10 What is the name of the opening and closing sections in a raga performance?

6 Introduction to composition

Objectives

In this chapter you will learn:

about the different requirements of the two composing units

various ways of approaching composition.

Introduction

You will be composing music for both Unit 2 (Composing and Appraising) and Unit 4 (Composing). The two compositions you write will together be worth 40 per cent of the final total for this examination: Unit 2 is worth 10 per cent and Unit 4 is worth 30 per cent. Each composition will be based on the elements of music which form the Areas of Study (AoS), which were covered in Chapter 2.

This chapter will look at different approaches to composing, and how to base compositions on the AoS. It will cover:

- what you have to do for the two composing units
- first approaches to composition.

What you have to do

The compositions

For both Unit 2 (Composing and Appraising Music) and Unit 4 (Composing Music), you are to compose a piece of music based on at least two of the Areas of Study (AoS).

Activity

1   Turn back to chapter 2 on pages 14–41 and look at the different Areas of Study.

■ Do you understand all the elements of music that are listed?

■ If not, check the ones you are not sure about with your teacher.

Your composition does not have to be any particular length, but look at the mark scheme for each unit (given on page 91): your music must show the full range of features to gain the higher marks. In a very short piece, it is unlikely that you will be able to include all of these and fully develop your musical ideas.

You must record your compositions and submit them with a score (see page 114) with **different compositions for each of the units**.

Each composition will be assessed against your choice of AoS as well as your use of the musical aspects. The main criteria are:

■ the imaginative use of sound

■ a sense of musical balance – for example, does your composition have a sense of beginning, middle and end?

■ the creation and development of musical ideas

■ an understanding of the chosen medium (the style of piece you are composing)

■ the appropriate and **idiomatic** use of instruments, voices and other sound sources

■ the appropriate use of musical elements, devices, techniques and **conventions**.

The differences between Units 2 and 4

Your composition for Unit 2 must link to one of the three strands. These are:

■ The Western Classical tradition

■ Popular music of the 20th and 21st centuries

■ World music.

In Unit 2, the examination board will decide on the strand for each year, but you choose from the styles and genres within it.

In Unit 4, you can choose to compose in *any* style or genre.

Key terms

Idiomatic: written in a way that sounds and feels natural for the instrument or voice.

Convention: something that is often done within a particular style or genre – for example, the use of the *tierce de Picardie* in baroque music.

Activity

2   Within each strand, there are many styles and genres from which to choose. Look at where the three strands are explained on pages 42–43.

■ Name a piece of music from each style or genre within the strand you have been studying.

■ What about the others?

■ Is there a style or genre you have never come across before? If so, ask your teacher to suggest some music to listen to.

The appraisal

In Unit 2 you will need to appraise your composition, commenting on the *process* of composition as well as the finished piece. An appraisal booklet will be provided and, on the inside cover, there will be questions based on the bullet points in the specification. These ask you to give:

- details of the two AoS you chose
- an explanation of *why* you chose these elements for your composition
- details of the process of composition and how you achieved the final recording
- comments on what makes the composition successful in terms of the AoS and strand chosen
- an explanation of how the composition relates to its context within the strand.

Your final compositions and Unit 2 appraisal will be done under 'controlled time' (see pages 146–7).

A *Appraising your composition*

Approaching composition

Some find composition easy; others find it extremely difficult. Often, the hardest part is simply getting started, having that all-important initial idea. Throughout the GCSE course, keep a 'composer's notebook': jot down any ideas for compositions that occur to you, even if you cannot think what to do with them at the time!

Ideas might include an occasion, a mood, a few notes, a rhythm, some lyrics, a chord progression, a bass riff: write them down and remember: *never throw away an idea*.

Use the form of notation easiest for you – staff notation, tab, a sequence of letters to represent pitches. Indicate rhythms – just showing the number of beats might be a start. For example:

A	A	B	C	A	F'	D'	E'
1	½	½	1	1	1	1	2

In staff notation, this becomes:

The same rhythm might be written as:

dum di-di dum dum dum dum daa-aa

Most of you will have written short pieces during Key Stage 3, and the techniques you learned then still apply. If you play an instrument, use this to work out your ideas (with your 'composer's notebook' close by). Most of you will have used a keyboard: this will be helpful. Writing ideas down might be difficult at first, but persevere.

Exam hints and tips

Compositions will be based on two or more of the AoS, thus including four or more of the elements of music.

Compositions will be judged on your use of the chosen elements and the success of the 'musical aspects':

- the imaginative use of sound
- a sense of musical balance
- the creation and development of musical ideas
- an understanding of the chosen medium
- the appropriate and idiomatic use of instruments, voices and other sound sources
- the appropriate use of musical elements, devices, techniques and conventions.

Objectives

You will learn:

how to prepare to compose

how to start a composition

how to write your ideas down

how the different elements can influence the style of your composition.

Did you know ??????

Beethoven produced many musical notebooks, which show his ideas developing over time.

These will be explained in the chapters that follow, and suggestions given as to how to use them in compositions. When preparing to compose and develop your compositions, listen to as wide a range of music as possible to understand how composers used these musical aspects in their compositions.

Activity

Remember an earlier composition of which you were proud.

■ List how it used the elements of music.

■ Why did you like it?

■ Why was it successful?

Planning your composition

Plan your composition carefully, deciding on:

■ rhythm – aim for variety; don't forget to use rests

■ metre – how many beats in a bar? Will this change?

■ harmony – in compositions for voices and/or pitched instruments, the use of chords and chord progressions will be vital

■ tonality – choice of key and/or scale affects the mood of your music

■ texture – aim for variety of textures

■ melody – usually a very important feature, worth taking time and care to make it memorable

■ timbre – which instruments/voices will you use?

■ dynamics – very important and can be very dramatic. *Silence* can also be very effective!

■ tempo – speed affects your music's mood and suitability for your intention. Will the tempo change?

■ structure and form – this *must* be thought about in advance to achieve balance and a sense of completeness.

C *Famous pianists and composers: (from top left) Handel, Bach, Weber, Beethoven, Mendelssohn-Bartholdy, Thalberg, Schumann, Schumann, Moscheles, Mozart*

6

This introduction has explained what you will have to do in composing, and given some tips and hints.

In this chapter you have learnt:

✔ to keep a composer's notebook for all your ideas

✔ to use the form of notation you find easiest – but remember you must be able to show pitch and rhythm

✔ to never throw an idea away

✔ to look back at earlier compositions and learn from them

✔ that your compositions have to be based on at least two of the Areas of Study

✔ that each Area of Study contains two elements of music

✔ to remember the differences between what you have to do for Unit 2 and Unit 4

✔ that you have to appraise your composition for Unit 2

✔ that if you play an instrument, you should use it when working out musical ideas

✔ that you should listen to as wide a range of music as possible.

Revision quiz

1 Complete the following Areas of Study:
   - AoS1: rhythm and ?
   - AOS2: ? and tonality
   - AOS3: ? and melody
   - AoS4: timbre & ?
   - AoS5: ? and form

2 What are the three Strands of Learning?

3 Which composition unit contains an appraisal?

4 How many AoS must you combine for your composition as a minimum?

5 Is there a minimum length for your composition?

6 What are the 'musical aspects'?

7 What do you have to do in the appraisal?

Objectives

In this chapter you will learn:

about the five Areas of Study

how to approach composition through each AoS

how to combine two or more AoS within your composition

how to combine instruments and/or voices for your composition

about the possible roles of ICT within composition

how best to decide on an appropriate type of composition

the range of ways of notating your composition

about linking compositions to the three Strands of Learning

how other composers have used the elements of music in their compositions.

■ Introduction

This chapter will take you through the process of composing, using the elements of music as your starting point. It will take a close look at each of the five Areas of Study and how these might be used within a composition, as well as referring to how they have been used by other composers. There will be tips and advice on how to start and then develop your composition, with suggestions for listening activities.

Musical elements: rhythm and metre (AoS1)

Rhythm

This refers to the use of notes of different lengths (durations) and the organisation of notes into patterns or rhythmic units or cells. You will already have learnt the different note names and their relative durations.

Activities

1   Check that you know the names, shapes and values of notes from the semibreve to the semiquaver (see page 186).

2   Work out the value of each of these five notes when a dot has been added.

3   Do these 'musical sums':

4   Work out some more sums with a partner.

Remember

The 'beat' is the regular pulse of the music, but the 'rhythm' will vary, using notes of different lengths to produce different patterns or groups of notes.

Metre

Metre is to do with the number of beats in each bar. A 'bar' is a unit or division of rhythm. Most music has the same number of *beats* in each bar (though not the same number of *notes* as this is more to do with *rhythm*). Metre is shown by the **time signature** at the beginning of the music. A time signature has two numbers: the top one shows how many beats there are in each bar; the bottom one shows which sort of note the beat is.

In this example from Chapter 6, the time signature is 4/4:

The top number means there are *four* beats in each bar; the bottom number means the beat is a *quarter note* or *crotchet*.

Activity

5   What do these time signatures mean? (If you are unsure, ask your teacher for help.)

3/4   2/4   5/4   2/2   6/8   9/8   7/16   4/1   3/2

Rhythm is an important feature of any composition, whether or not pitched notes are used. Tap or clap these rhythmic ideas. Ask for help if you need it.

Work with other players and perform these rhythms in any order you want, repeating any bar as many times as you want.

Now try 'shifting' a simple rhythm. For example, use the second half of a well-known rhythmic pattern:

Now add in an extra crotchet beat to form this pattern:

Or miss off the last crotchet, giving:

In a group of three people, perform these three rhythms together by clapping, tapping or playing the lines on percussion instruments. After how many bars would you all be back to the start of your rhythms at the same time?

Research study

Music based on rhythm and metre

Listen to the rhythms of African and Caribbean music.

Listen to music by John Adams and Steve Reich.

Listen to 'Take five' or 'Unsquare dance' by Dave Brubeck.

Listening activity

6   Work out your own starting rhythm and then add and take away beats to form new patterns.

Get a group of students to play them, and listen carefully to the effects you can achieve.

Alternatively, you could multi-track the rhythms using ICT.

Listen to track 31 on the CD: adding a 7-beat version means the patterns come together on the first beat of bar 106, after 3 minutes at 140 bpm!

7.2 Musical elements: harmony and tonality (AoS2)

Harmony

Harmony can be divided into two main types:

Functional – where two or more different notes are sounded together in a way that has some structural significance.

Non-functional – where the combination of notes is used for its immediate effect rather than as part of a progression or sequence.

Most music uses *functional* harmony, and is often based on a sequence or progression of chords, with a real sense of logic in the way one chord moves (or resolves) to the next.

Objectives

You will learn:

about the meaning of 'harmony' and 'tonality'

about how these elements can be used in your composition

about how other composers have used these elements.

Activity

1 Using a chord sequence can be a good way to start a composition.

Look at this example of the chords built on each note of the major scale with their names and Roman numerals:

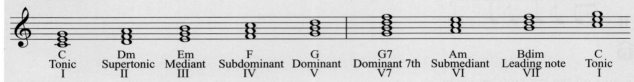

C	Dm	Em	F	G	G7	Am	Bdim	C
Tonic	Supertonic	Mediant	Subdominant	Dominant	Dominant 7th	Submediant	Leading note	Tonic
I	II	III	IV	V	V7	VI	VII	I

You can build chords in this way in any key, and then combine them in sequences. For example, try:

■ I VI IV V (in C major, that would be C Am F G)

■ I IV V I (or C F G C)

■ the 12-bar blues sequence: I I I I | IV IV I I | V7 IV7 I I or V7 (C C C C | F F C C | G7 F7 C C or G7).

In each of these examples, each chord lasts a full bar.

There are many ways of using these chords:

■ strum them on a guitar

■ play them on a keyboard

■ record them or get somebody else to record them

Then try to work out a short tune to fit with them.

You should try to organise your music into regular phrases, or have a recognisable group of notes (or **hook**).

Decide whether your music will start in a *major* key or a *minor* key, remembering that this choice will affect the mood of your music. Decide on the number of beats in a bar and on the speed (*tempo*) of your composition.

The chords given are **diatonic**. When you are comfortable with using these, you should experiment with others, and with **dissonance**.

Key terms

Hook: a short, memorable musical idea played regularly and/or sung to a main word or phrase.

Diatonic: containing the notes from a major or minor scale.

Dissonance: sounds which clash when played together.

■ Tonality

Most music is **tonal**, based in a clearly defined key. Some composers have experimented with:

- *bi-tonality* (two keys together)
- *polytonality* (many keys together)
- *atonality* (no key).

You will probably have learnt something about keys and scales, and can use words such as *major*, *minor*, *modal*, *pentatonic*, and possibly others.

For this AoS, you need only use *major* or *minor* keys or *modes*, though you should listen to music which uses other keys and scales.

As you compose and plan how your piece will develop, you will need to think about whether to change key (*modulate*) or not. Moving into a different key is like a journey, where you enter a different sound area. It is often very effective, and can also provide direction for your music, as can the return journey to the original or home key.

Modulation can be to the subdominant (IV) or dominant (V) or to the relative minor (from a major key) or the relative major (from a minor key). Key changes to the subdominant or dominant need a change of scale as there will be one note different between the two keys: for example, to modulate from C major to F major needs the replacement of B with B flat. (More on modulation on page 23.)

(More on modulation on page 23.)

> **Did you know ??????**
>
> You can use this sentence to remember the order in which sharps are added: Father Charles Goes Down And Ends Battle. Reversing it gives the order of flats: Battle Ends And Down Goes Charles' Father.

Activity

2 Play these examples of scales. First, a major scale:

Next, different versions of a minor scale:

Harmonic

Now you have tried chord sequences in major keys, you can try writing music with a *modal* feel, by using Am G F G or Em D C D as progressions. Here are the two modes to use:

■ Texture

This refers to how many different lines of music are heard at the same time, and also the type of music they have. It can range from a single line to a very complex texture where many different things are happening at the same time. This can be heard in music for large groups of players or singers.

A single-line melody is the simplest texture you can use. You can move on, as you gain in confidence, to add other instruments, thus thickening the texture. You could add a piano or guitar part to your tune (melody with accompaniment), write another tune to go with it (a countermelody), add a drone or an ostinato, harmonise each note to produce a harmonic or homophonic texture, or have many different ideas going on at the same time, creating a contrapuntal or polyphonic texture.

■ Melody

A melody, or tune, is a series of notes, organised into a pattern of rhythms and pitches to produce a musical shape that may become memorable.

It will normally contain a mixture of movement by step and by leap, and the range of notes used will depend on the instrument or voice chosen.

A melody can be any length, but often breaks down into two- or four-bar phrases. There will often be repetition of some phrases or ideas, especially in longer pieces.

You might find it easier to think of writing a tune as working with questions and answers, where the first phrase (the question) sounds unfinished and the second phrase (the answer) completes it and balances it.

If the two-bar phrase from page 92 is the question, it might be *answered* like this:

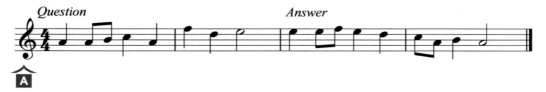

Here, the opening *question* rises from A to E, sounding unfinished, while the balancing *answer* falls from the E and ends on the A, making the whole musical sentence sound complete and finished.

Melodies can be based on triads, can be diatonic, chromatic, pentatonic, even whole tone, and you should experiment with many different short pieces, keeping your ideas in your composer's notebook. Your ideas can be reversed (**retrograde**), turned upside down (**inverted**), used in a **sequence**: there are so many different things you can try while preparing for the main compositions you will be writing.

Key terms

Sequence: the repetition of a phrase at a higher or lower pitch.

Listening activities

2   Write a melody which starts with a triad, as in this example from Beethoven's Piano Sonata no. 4, op. 7:

3   Write a melody which uses lots of chromatic notes, as in the theme music to the James Bond films, or the Harry Lime theme from the film *The Third Man*.

4   Write a melody using the whole tone scale, as in this example from Bartók's First String Quartet (the sign ✕, placed in front of a note, indicates a double sharp, where the pitch of the note is raised by two semitones):

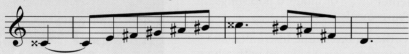

5   Listen to Debussy's Piano Prelude *Voiles* on the CD track 32: a piece written using the whole tone scale.

A *Bartók*

B *Debussy*

C *Beethoven*

Remember

Keep your ideas in your composer's notebook, coming back to them from time to consider ways of extending and improving them.

■ Timbre

There are many terms which you need to be aware of when thinking about this element: refer to them on pages 30–35.

Timbre is to do with the sounds of different instruments and voices. Your choice of timbre will greatly affect the mood of your music. Think of the opening of the film *Jaws*: much of the effect is gained through the use of very low sounds. Imagine those same notes played on a glockenspiel or a flute! There would be no sense of fear, of expectation, of danger.

Most instruments can produce a wide range of notes and, often, the timbre will change as it moves from low notes to high notes. Listen to the music for the cat, from *Peter and the Wolf* by Prokofiev, for a good example of use of the lower register, the *chalumeau* register of the clarinet. Listen to parts of Mozart's Clarinet Quintet for how he uses the whole range of the clarinet. Listen to the range of effects that Vivaldi gets from the violin in *The Four Seasons* (*Le Quattro Stagioni*).

Listen to combinations of different timbres in string quartets, in concertos, in music for voices, whether *lieder* or modern pop songs, both for single voice and with backing vocals.

Instrumental techniques may affect the timbre. Some instruments can be muted; orchestral string instruments can be played with a bow (*con arco*) or the strings can be plucked (*pizzicato*).

Activities

1. Find someone who can play a brass instrument. Ask them to play a tune and then play it again with a mute fitted: listen to the different effects.

2. Find someone who can play a bowed string instrument. Ask them to play a tune using the bow, then to repeat it playing *pizzicato*. Compare the effects.

Timbre also refers to the sounds produced by technology, such as electronic keyboards and synthesisers; it also covers the way technology can alter sounds by distorting them, adding reverb and chorus effects. These timbres are often evident in pop song recordings, such as those by Pink Floyd, Genesis, Soft Cell and many others.

Activity

3. If you have access to music software, experiment with inputting a short melody and then altering its sound by using distortion, reverb and chorus.

Objectives

You will learn:

the meaning of 'timbre'

how timbre can be used effectively in your compositions

how other composers have used timbre

the meaning of 'dynamics'

how dynamics can be used effectively in your compositions

how other composers have used dynamics.

A *Trumpet (not muted)*

B *Trumpet (muted)*

■ Dynamics

This refers to changes in volume: these can be gradual or sudden. The range of dynamics and dynamic effects can be found on pages 34–35: refer to them as you need to or to refresh your memory.

The range of dynamics and dynamic effects can be found on pages 34–35

> **Listening activity**
>
> Listen to examples of film music where changing dynamics is a major element. Such changes usually accompany a change of scene or mood, or warn you that something is about to happen. In film music, silence can be very effective, too.
>
> Listen to the music of *Star Wars*, *Atonement* or *Gladiator* and notice how dynamics are used to set or change the mood.

Loud music tends to be triumphant or happy, used at parties and celebrations, for action. Quiet music can be sad, thoughtful, dreamy, used for times of reflection, at funerals, for moments of peace and calm.

Compare the different moods of the loud opening of Haydn's Trumpet Concerto in E♭ and its quieter, more peaceful slow movement, or the Beatles' 'She loves you' with the contrasts within Led Zeppelin's 'Stairway to Heaven'.

C *Think about how these different instruments can evoke different moods*

Structure and form

Having got started with your composition, you will need to think carefully about how it is going to develop. This will involve planning its structure or form.

In some cases, you might decide to write a piece of music which has a set form, such as music in binary, ternary, rondo or theme and variations form. For explanations of these and other structures and forms, refer to pages 36–41.

Some forms are more flexible, such as cyclic form, sonata form, popular song form and through-composed music.

Binary form is the simplest, consisting of two sections in similar style. Often, the first section ends with a modulation (change of key); the second section returns to the original or home key and ends firmly in that key. Usually, each section is played twice.

Adapting the opening idea already used in these chapters, a binary form piece could look like this: the first 4 bars have been extended to 8 bars, and modulate to C major (the relative major); the second section begins in C major before returning to the original idea from bar 13 and finishing the piece firmly in A minor:

Objectives

You will learn:

about different structures and forms

how these can be used effectively in your compositions

how other composers have used structure and form.

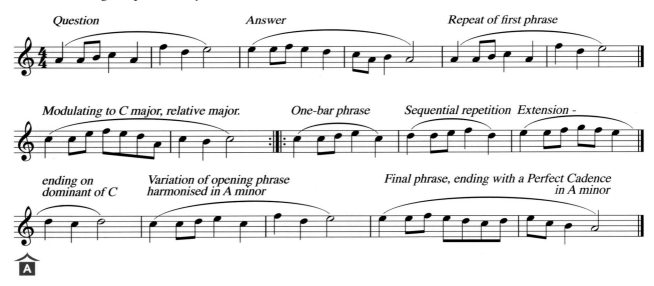

Ternary form would mean writing a contrasting middle section of music and then playing your first section again (with or without repeats). The contrast could be of key, tempo, dynamics, the style of the music, the pitches used, the timbre or texture and so on.

Rondo form requires a very strong main section (A) as this will be heard several times, contrasting with other sections (B, C and so on), to make a structure like A B A C A D A. Arch-shape is a different version of rondo form: A B C B A.

Key terms

Middle 8: term given to the contrasting section in a pop song, usually (but not necessarily) eight bars long. See page 67.

Listening activities

1 Listen to some songs by the Beatles, including 'Love me do', 'She loves you' and 'A day in the life'. Work out their different forms.

2 Listen to songs by other singers or bands, and present your findings to other members of your group.

3 Listen to the *Canon* by Pachelbel or Coolio's 'I'll C U when U get there', both based on the same ground bass:

Using this ground bass, write your own set of variations to fit with it. You will need to think carefully about which chords fit with the ground bass notes: Pachelbel's *Canon* is in D major, and he uses the chords shown in the example above.

B *The Beatles*

Research study

Sonata form

Look up the details of sonata form (see page 39).

Its alternative name is **first movement form**: look at how composers have modified this form in their compositions, and present your findings to your group.

Useful websites: **www.wikipedia.org   www.answers.yahoo.com**

Try searching on 'sonata form'.

Next look for articles on 'sonata' alone – what information can you find out about the links between the two?

When writing a song, the simplest form is **strophic**, where each verse is set to the same music: there are many examples in *lieder* and folk music. The most complicated is **through-composed**, where the music changes with the text or lyrics: examples include 'The Erl King' by Schubert and 'Bohemian rhapsody' by Queen. Popular songs often use a **verse and chorus** structure, sometimes with a contrasting **Middle 8**.

The Beatles experimented with many different song forms, from the simplicity of 'Love me do' to the more complex pieces on the *Sergeant Pepper's Lonely Hearts Club Band* album of 1967.

As you experiment with compositions, try out different forms and structures. This will affect the length of your composition: while a pop song can quite happily fit into about three minutes, a binary or ternary form piece might be shorter. On the other hand, pieces in rondo form, or using theme and variations or sonata form, might need to be longer than this.

7.6 The elements combined

The focus of the composition

The two compositions you complete have to be based on at least two of the AoS. Each AoS is made up of two of the elements of music, so there are many possible combinations.

Combining AoS1 (rhythm and metre) with AoS4 (timbre and dynamics) opens up many possibilities for composition. Much of the piece could be based on a series of ostinato patterns using different combinations of instruments. You might start by building up an underlying rhythmic pattern with a range of percussion instruments. You could base the rhythms on rock music, create an Indian feel or conjure up a Caribbean beat. Add in a bass riff and then further ostinato patterns using instruments of your choice and creating different textures.

Dynamics can be brought into play through contrast and through gradual gradation.

As your piece progresses, you will be conscious of using other elements to some extent, such as structure and form, texture and tempo. Although careful use of these will help with the overall balance and success of the composition, the main focus of the assessment will be on how you have used your chosen four elements.

Objectives

You will learn:

how two or more of the AoS can be combined to create an effective composition

how other composers have successfully combined the elements of music.

Activity

Write a piece of music using the outline given above.

Before you start, decide on the time signature, tempo, and the instruments you will be using.

As you make progress, decide on its form.

Your piece should have a clear sense of shape, perhaps:

- introduction – where you establish the rhythm and bass riff
- first main section – where more ostinato patterns are added including one with a recognisable pattern or hook
- middle section – where the texture is reduced and the rhythm becomes prominent again, perhaps varied slightly
- second main section – where some of the earlier ostinato patterns return but some are new or varied
- final section – rounding off the piece.

Think carefully about how you will use dynamics for contrast and variety.

You might decide to combine AoS2 (harmony and tonality) with AoS5 (structure and form) and write a piece for instruments and/or voices using either a set form or establishing a clear form of your own.

You could decide to write a popular song using this form:

- intro
- verse 1
- chorus
- verse 2
- chorus
- middle 8 or bridge
- instrumental verse
- chorus
- chorus in a new key (usually a tone or semitone higher than the original)
- outro/ending.

The intro needs to be memorable; many pop songs start with a bass riff or a repeated phrase. Listen to some pop songs for a range of ideas.

The chorus is very important: it will usually contain the melody which most people will focus on, so it needs to be catchy, possibly with a hook on a key word or phrase. What is the most memorable feature of your favourite songs?

The verse needs to contrast with the chorus, and often tells the story or sets the scene.

A change of key for the last chorus will give the music a lift and provide contrast.

Think carefully of the instruments you will use, and who will be singing the words. Will you use a rock band line-up of three guitars and drums? Will you use keyboards/synthesisers? Will you use a sequencer to provide the backing? The words or lyrics are also important: you could use existing words, or new ones.

A *Keyboard player*

7.7 Instrumental and vocal combinations

Using instruments

If you are writing for instruments, you have many choices to make:

- Will you use tuned or untuned instruments or a combination?
- Will you use a single instrument, a small group of instruments or a large group?
- Will there be a main instrument with an accompaniment?
- Will you use orchestral instruments, pop instruments or electronic instruments?

Using untuned instruments will rely on percussion instruments and their availability but, of course, these can be from the orchestra, from popular music, or from African, Caribbean or Indian music.

Using tuned instruments makes the choice very wide indeed, including both acoustic and electronic sound-sources.

If you write a piece of music for a single instrument, you should choose one that you can play, or one you know a lot about, and can find someone who plays it to ask for advice.

If you are going to write for a small group, there are several established instrumental groupings such as the string quartet, wind quintet, piano trio and so on, though you could simply choose your own small group from people you know.

Larger groups would cover jazz bands, orchestras, wind ensembles, string orchestras, brass bands and so on.

You might write for a solo instrument accompanied by piano or guitar.

Another consideration is the *type* of instrument, whether from the string, woodwind, brass or percussion families, or from the world of pop music and technology.

Try out a few different combinations of instruments to find the one you think you can work with best. When you have decided, you should write several short pieces for your chosen combination and fully research their capabilities, preferably consulting people who can play them.

Listening activity

Listen to the following pieces:

- *Canon and Gigue* by Pachelbel
- Spring, Summer, Autumn or Winter from *The Four Seasons* by Vivaldi
- Slow movement from the Trumpet Concerto in E♭ by Haydn
- 'The Erl King' by Schubert
- 'Nessun dorma' from *Turandot* by Puccini
- 'She loves you' by the Beatles
- 'Bohemian rhapsody' by Queen
- 'Tainted love' by Soft Cell
- 'Stairway to Heaven' by Led Zeppelin
- Fourth (variations) movement of the 'Trout' Quintet by Schubert
- Excerpts from the sound track to *Star Wars* by John Williams and/or *Lord of the Rings* by Howard Shore
- Excerpts from *The Rough Guide to the Music of India*

Discuss the ways in which composers have made use of the characteristics of instruments, voices and technology within these compositions.

Using voices

Music for voices can be for a single voice (usually with some sort of accompaniment) through small ensembles to full choirs. It includes pop songs with backing vocals and close harmony groups.

If you sing in a rock band, a group or a choir, you will have experience of what works well for the voice and will be able to bring this to bear when composing. It is very important that the range of the chosen voices is kept in mind: if you are writing for particular singers, be aware of what will be comfortable for them to sing and try not to stray outside this range.

If you enjoy singing, you might decide to sing your song yourself and, if you can, add backing vocals by using a multi-track recorder.

Research study

Listen to a range of music written for voices including 'Nessun dorma' by Puccini, *Carmina Burana* by Carl Orff, blues music, the Beatles, the Rolling Stones, songs and choruses from musicals, and recent pop music. Take careful note of how the different composers have used the voice, and listen carefully to the different styles of voice.

Activity

Write a short piece of music for one or more voices, accompanied or unaccompanied. The important thing is to learn about what the voice can do and hear your song sung by yourself and others. Better to complete a short section at this stage than a whole song.

A *Voices used in a choir*

You can use ICT as a tool for composition or simply as a means of realising your music.

Multi-track recording

Using a multi-track recorder enables you to build up your composition one track at a time, which is particularly useful if you are performing all the tracks or want to combine acoustic, sequenced and computer-generated sounds. It means you can record your music in stages, checking its accuracy, setting dynamic levels, adding effects such as reverb or chorus, and finally mixing and panning the final piece before saving it as a stereo recording.

Multi-track recorders are being updated all the time, so it is best to seek advice if intending to purchase one. Useful websites might include

- **www.tascam.com**
- **www.wikipedia.org** (search on 'multi-track recording').

Some keyboards also allow you to produce multi-track recordings, though without some of the effects available through acoustic input. You could refer to the manufacturers' websites for help. For example, the Yamaha site at:

- **www.yamaha.com**

has a 'knowledge base' section with information about all the Yamaha musical equipment.

A *Multi-track recorder*

Computer software

Many computer software programs make it easy to input many instrumental lines: these include Finale, Notator and Sibelius. They enable you to choose from a wide range of instruments and play the parts in **real** or **step time**.

The quality of the recorded sound will depend on the sound card used. Alternatively, you can choose to save the composition as a MIDI file and export it before realisation.

Objectives

You will learn:

about the use of ICT in producing effective compositions

how other composers have used ICT effectively in their compositions.

Activity

1 Experiment with using a multi-track recorder:

Either by yourself or with others, record at least three tracks of music, adjusting dynamics and panning as appropriate.

Key terms

Real time: playing the music into the computer and it records the actual rhythms that you play.

Step time: inputting the notes one at a time, choosing the duration and pitch of each in turn.

Activity

2 If you have access to one of these software programs, use it to set up a score by
- adding instruments
- setting a time signature
- choosing a key and
- setting the tempo.

Then input some music, either in real or step time, and play it back. On Sibelius, for example, you can add phrasing, dynamics, articulation and other effects to improve the quality of the playback.

Research study

Multi-track recording

Find out how 'Being for the benefit of Mr Kite' from *Sergeant Pepper's Lonely Hearts Club Band* by the Beatles was recorded, and make a presentation of your findings to the group, demonstrating how the hardware and software available in your school can be used to achieve similar results.

The sequencer

Programs such as Logic and Cubase allow you to enter music in real or step time and open up the possibility of playing your music in through another instrument. However, it is more difficult to produce an accurate score with these programs – though not impossible.

Cubase and Sibelius are probably the most widely used programs though, as a sequencing package, Acoustica Mixcraft has many good features.

You could search on Google to find information on the various programs. Find out what you have available at school, and go to that company's website to find out more about it.

If you have access to one of these programs, use it to play in some music as set out in the activity above.

The secret to gaining good quality input and recordings is practice. If you think that one of these approaches would be good for you, work at many short exercises, gradually deciding which type of composition you will write and what resources you will use.

Recording studios have the facilities to lay down many tracks and most, if not all, pop bands work in this way to produce their recordings.

Remember, however, that technology cannot replace good musical ideas: it is your composition that will gain the marks!

B *Cubase software*

What to compose

During music lessons before starting your GCSE course, you will most likely have composed music both on your own and with others. For GCSE, any composition submitted must be entirely your own work or, where it isn't, you must explain in full what you have done, and what others have done.

It is quite likely that you might already have found an area of composing that appeals to you and that you are confident with: this is good, but should not stop you experimenting as much as possible at first. If you play an instrument or sing regularly, this may be the best way into composition. At first, you will probably be doing some exercises in composition to improve what you can do and introduce you to new techniques and new musical language. However, it is important that when you come to decide on your final compositions, you are able to approach the main building blocks – the elements of music – with confidence and know that you will enjoy the process of composition.

Choice of Area of Study

For both compositions, you must choose at least two of the AoS (and, therefore, four elements). Your first decision must be, therefore, which AoS will appeal to you most, and enable you to compose a successful piece of music.

For Unit 2 (Composing and Appraising Music), you must also link your composition to one of the three strands:

- The Western Classical tradition
- Popular music of the 20th and 21st centuries
- World music.

For more information on these strands, see chapters 3–5.

Your own interests and abilities should always pay a large part in your decisions regarding what to compose. What types of music do you like to listen to? What types of music do you perform? You should aim to harness your experience as both a listener and a performer to help you in your compositions.

There are many questions you should ask yourself as you decide which AoS to combine. These include:

- Am I good at writing melodies?
- Am I good at harmony?
- Do I enjoy working with rhythm?
- Do I want to work with different timbres?
- Do I want to base my composition on an existing structure or form?
- Do I want to work with more than one instrument and vary textures?

Answering these questions will help you focus on the two AoS which will be best for you.

Objectives

You will learn:

how to choose the appropriate type of composition

how to choose the most appropriate resources.

Remember

The five Areas of Study: if necessary, refer to them on pages 14–41 and pages 98–107.

The six musical aspects: if necessary, refer to these on page 90.

■ Resources

Decisions on what to compose should also be influenced by the resources available for hearing your music as it develops, checking its suitability for the instruments/voices chosen and creating a final performance.

You might choose to write music that you will perform either on a single instrument or by multi-tracking. You might look to an existing group of players/singers and write for them. You might decide that, as you are part of a rock band (or other small group) and have experience writing for them already, you will make this the focus of your compositions.

The important thing always is to write to your strengths. Your talents and abilities can be improved over quite a large part of this GCSE course before you actually need to start planning and composing your final pieces.

A   *What sort of music do you want to compose and for whom?*

7.10 Writing it down

Why notate your music?

In an examination, it is important that you submit a score as well as a recording of your composition, so that the people assessing your work can fully understand your intentions in case they do not come across clearly in the recorded performance. Remember that it is the composition itself that is being assessed: the performance is an aid for you, your teacher and the moderator to make sure that what is heard is what is meant.

Objectives

You will learn:

the different ways of notating your compositions

how to decide which method is best for you

what is expected within this examination.

Types of notation

There are several ways of writing down your composition:

- staff notation
- graphic notation
- tab
- a written account detailing the structure and content of the music
- a combination of some or all of these.

It is very important that, whichever method you choose, your score accurately reflects what you were trying to express in your compositions, and that it is easy for other people to follow and understand your music from what you present.

Staff notation

This is the traditional method of notating music and, in many ways, is the most precise, as it gives actual pitches and rhythms as well as allowing you to put in the time signature, tempo, and many performance and expressive details. A line of music such as this gives the player and listener a lot of information:

There is precise detail on tempo, key, phrasing, use of dynamics and the *legato* style required. If you can use this form of notation, it should certainly be your first option.

Graphic notation

As the name suggests, this form of notation involves substituting pictures and/or symbols for sounds. By its nature, it is less precise than staff notation and will always need additional information in terms of a key to the pictures/symbols used, addition of speed, phrasing and dynamic markings, some way of indicating duration such as a time line, and so on.

Tab

Tab is very much favoured by guitarists and exists in two main forms: one which simply indicates the pitch of each note by showing which fret on which string is to be played:

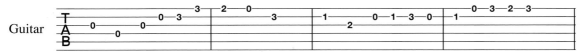

or one with slightly more detail, indicating rhythms as well:

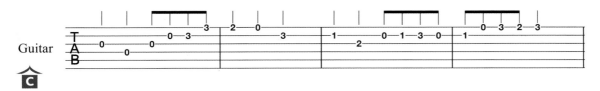

Further information in terms of tempo, dynamics, style of playing and phrasing would all be needed.

A written account detailing the structure and content of the music

This method can be very useful but *must* really be written alongside the composition. You will need to describe in detail what your music is doing and what can be heard. Preferably, your account should be broken down into timings linked to specific, clearly audible events in your music. You will need to give details of instruments, tempo, form and so on, so that anyone listening to your music can follow the sounds and link them easily to your stated intentions in the account.

D *Composing music*

Combining some or all of these

Combining elements from some or all of these methods of notation might be a good compromise for many. As well as the written account, there could be short musical quotations of melodic and/or rhythmic ideas, tab patterns, and some graphics with clear explanations.

The final choice will depend on your ability in notation, but you must submit your recording of your composition with a musical score in one of the formats outlined above.

7.11 Writing it down: staff notation and graphic notation

Staff notation

Staff notation is precise and is universally read and understood. Wherever possible, it should be your first choice as it allows you to put in so much detail very concisely. Consider this example:

A

The instrumentation is shown: clarinet and piano. It sets the tempo (72 bpm) and the style (*Andante cantabile* – at a moderate speed and songlike); the opening dynamic is indicated – **mf** (*mezzo forte* or quite loud) – and then gradations of dynamic are shown. The key is shown – F minor. In the final bar, the pianist is instructed to use the sustaining pedal, lifting off at the end of the bar. The precise notes, rhythm and phrasing are shown, all much more concisely than could be explained in other ways.

This second example is from Beethoven's Piano Sonata no. 4, last movement, *Rondo*:

B

The key is E♭ major; the tempo and style – *Poco Allegretto e grazioso* – translates as *Somewhat fast and gracefully*. The dynamic and subsequent shading are clear to see; there is **staccato** articulation for the right hand of the piano on two occasions; **sf** or *sforzando* is shown, meaning to accent or stress the notes marked; there are phrase marks for both hands, and a pause – *fermata* – on the last note of this example. Again, a lot of information given very concisely.

■ Graphic notation

This uses images and symbols to represent sounds.

Thus, these symbols might show a note repeated but played louder each time.

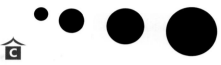

This pattern of lines might show the general pitch outline and relative lengths of a pattern of notes:

while this might show a group of three notes being played together:

and this a block or cluster of notes:

Other shapes could be used to represent a crash, its volume depending upon the size of the symbol:

A smoother melodic line might look like this:

Whatever symbols, signs and drawings you decide upon, you must provide a key to them, explaining what they mean and assigning them to an instrument or sound source, such as a handclap, a foot stamp and so on.

A time line should also be shown, indicating horizontally the duration of each section of music and, where more than one sound is to be heard simultaneously, the symbols should be arranged vertically.

Whatever range of drawings and symbols you use, a graphic score will always remain a somewhat imprecise method of showing your intentions, but it is certainly better than nothing.

Research study

Notations

Explore more about notations at:

www.wikipedia.org
www.google.com
www.answers.com

Try searching on 'music notation', 'staff notation' and/or 'graphic notation'.

Try to get hold of some scores of music by John Cage to see what notation he used in his compositions.

7.12 | Writing it down: tab and written account (annotation)

Tab

Tab notation is the preferred choice of most rock guitarists and bass players. Many websites exist where popular music can be obtained in tab form, and it is a useful form of notation. Its stave represents the six strings of an acoustic or electric guitar or the four strings of a bass guitar. It can accommodate tuning adjustments such as Drop D tuning, where the lowest-pitched string is tuned down to D instead of the usual E. As well as pitch, tab *can* indicate rhythm. If tab is to be used, this second method should be adopted as it gives more information. However, you will still need to find ways of showing tempo and articulation. Just how much will depend on what is contained in the score.

A tab score can include dynamics and devices including the use of **trills** and **pitch bend**.

It can show chords as well as a single melody line: consider these two examples:

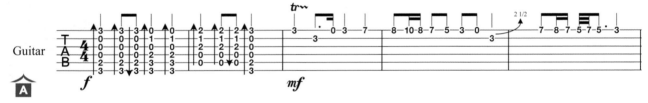

A

This example shows a chordal introduction, its dynamic (*f* meaning *forte* or loud) and the direction in which the chords are to be strummed. The dynamic drops to *mf* (*mezzo forte or fairly loud*) for the melody in bar 3, and there are indications for a trill (bar 3^1) and a pitch bend (bars 4^4– 5^1).

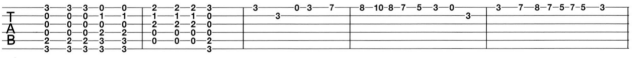

B

This is exactly the same music, but lacks much of the detail shown in the previous example, and would therefore need more written information.

Writing it down (annotation)

A written account to accompany a composition has always been an option at GCSE: such a written account or **annotation** must enable the listener to follow the music and understand the composer's intentions. Thus, it must be detailed and cover all aspects of the music heard. References to musical events within the composition that can easily be heard are usually the best way to approach this.

Consider these two openings to accounts of the same piece of music:

> ❝ *My music starts with a verse and then the main chorus comes in. I sing and accompany myself on guitar. The chords used are G Em C and D⁷. It is quite a happy song.* ❞

> ❝ *The song is called 'Here comes that boy again' and is about a boy I met at a party. We had a great time and I thought I would write this song to show just how happy we are. As well as singing, I play the guitar chords in the accompaniment. On a separate sheet are the lyrics of my song and the chords, showing where they change. It starts with a short introduction where I play G Em C D⁷ twice, strumming the chords in an up-beat rhythm in 4/4 and the key of G.* ❞

Although these are only the openings, it is obvious that the second account gives much more information and is of more use to those assessing the composition.

This should be your aim: a very detailed account, covering all aspects of your composition.

C *Play your piece to others*

Reasons for choosing a particular type of notation

This section will help you to choose between staff notation, graphic notation, tab, a written account or a combination of these.

Staff notation

This should be your first choice wherever possible, because it is so precise, it is universally understood and it will save a lot of writing! The more complex your piece of music, the easier it is for someone else to understand it if staff notation has been used.

Graphic notation

Graphic notation is useful but has serious limitations which mean it lacks precision and needs to be backed up with written details.

Tab

The form of tab which includes indications of rhythm and pitch plus performance and expressive detail is preferable, but even this will need to be accompanied by additional information.

A written account (annotation)

This is perfectly acceptable method of describing your composition, but you must ensure that it is very detailed. It should refer, where appropriate, to:

- rhythm
- metre
- harmony
- tonality
- texture
- melody
- timbre
- dynamics
- structure and form.

The drawback is that this can end up being very long.

A combination of some or all of the above

If you choose to use staff notation, you will need to do very little else except respond to what is asked for on the Candidate Record Form.

If you use any other method, you will need to include other things. For example, using **graphic notation** will need the addition of a key to the symbols, some sort of time line, indication of instruments and so on. Using **tab** will need more information to amplify what is given on the score. If you are in the position of being able to convert the tab

Objectives

You will learn:

how to use your chosen method effectively

how other composers have used these methods in their compositions.

notation into staff notation, this will certainly help a lot. A **written account/annotation** is improved by the inclusion of musical excerpts to help explain what is happening.

How to choose

Your initial choice, at least in the early stages of composing, will be determined by your ability. However, it should be stressed that a good working knowledge of staff notation is a great asset and will help in other areas of music, including performing and listening.

Whichever method you finally decide to adopt, make sure that you include full details of all your intentions as a composer. Even if your composition includes an element of improvisation, it is vital that the basis of that improvisation is clearly explained, be it a melodic or rhythmic idea, a chord progression, a particular scale, or whatever.

The vast majority of published music uses staff notation. Many pop musicians work with tab. Outside the examination situation, a written account of a composition just doesn't exist (though it is a completely acceptable option here).

Having explored different types of musical score, decide which has been the most concise and precise in giving its information. What additional information would other methods need?

A *Different types of musical score*

7.14 Listening and study: introduction

Listening to music

As you learn different techniques for composing, it is important to see how other composers have made successful use of them in their compositions. What you have learnt may be just one part of a composition, so you will need to concentrate on just that aspect of it. This will be easier with some techniques than with others but you will often be able to use the same piece of music to learn about the use of many different elements.

For example, if you are learning about the sound of a particular instrument, the best way of hearing how other composers have used it is to choose a piece where that instrument is featured, such as a **concerto**. But the music could lead you in other directions. For example, listening for the sound of the solo instruments can soon lead to listening for other musical elements that you might want to use in your own compositions.

How to improve your listening skills

When listening to a piece of music, especially at first, aim to concentrate on one particular feature of what you hear, playing the piece several times as you focus on how it has been used by the composer.

Put a heading to show the focus of your listening (e.g. timbre, rhythm, tonality) and then make notes as you listen: bullet points will do.

Make sure that you will be able to listen without interruption.

Always use good equipment for playback.

The examples on the CD include:

Objectives

You will learn:

how listening to music can help improve composition

what to listen to when preparing to compose

how to improve your listening skills

how to plan your listening.

Listening activity

1   Listen to the concerto excerpts on the CD tracks 33–35 and compare the ways in which the composers have:

■ written for the solo instruments

■ used tonality: the first two are in major keys, the third in the minor

■ used rhythm

■ used dynamics

■ used different textures.

Trumpet in E♭

A *Trumpet Concerto in E♭ by Haydn*

Key terms

Concerto: music written for a solo instrument and orchestra (see pages 48–51).

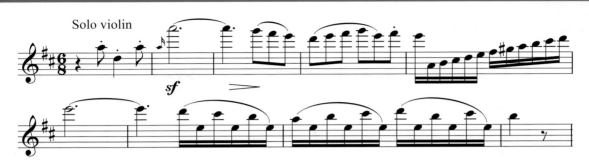

B *Violin Concerto in D major op. 61 by Beethoven*

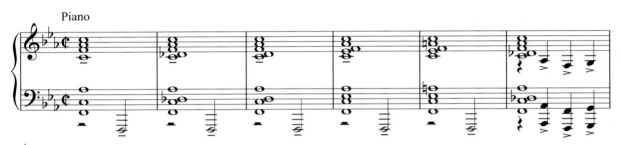

C *Piano Concerto no. 2 in C minor op. 18 by Rachmaninov*

How to plan your listening

For each area of listening, your teacher will be able to suggest pieces of music which will be relevant. Try to listen to as many of these as possible, covering as many different styles and genres of music as you can. Different composers, periods and traditions have different approaches to using each of the elements.

Using 'structure and form' as an example, you could be listening to a piece of music to hear a specific set form such as binary, ternary, rondo and so on in use.

- *Binary* is any music in two sections with each section in a similar style.
- *Ternary* has a contrasting central section: some think of it as 'sandwich form' with the bread on either side and a filling in the middle. It might be a da capo aria, where the singer sings section A, then the contrasting section B, and then repeats A, usually improvising a decoration of the melody.
- *Rondo* has a main tune alternating with contrasting episodes.

Popular and world music can be used to access a wide range of structures, timbres, rhythms and so on: ask your teacher for further ideas.

Listening activity

2   Listen to these pieces on the CD tracks 36–38, and see if you can hear where the different parts of the structure start and finish:

- Ternary form: 'The watchman's song' by Grieg

- Da capo aria: 'The trumpet shall sound' from *Messiah* by Handel, preceded by its introductory recitative

- Rondo form: Horn Concerto no. 4 in E♭ by Mozart, last movement.

7.15 Combinations of the musical elements

How to combine different elements

Before reading this section, refer to pages 106–107 (The elements combined). In that section, there were suggestions as to how AoS1 and 4, and AoS2 and 5 might lead to a composition. We will suggest two possible approaches combining AoS3 (texture and melody) with AoS5 (structure and form). There are many possibilities: here we will imagine a piece for wind ensemble and a piece for a pop-style group using synthesisers, guitars, vocals, and perhaps other instruments such as trumpets.

The pop-style group

Build up the opening texture gradually, starting with a riff on bass guitar alone, adding drums and synthesiser after four bars, using a chord sequence of Em, Am, Em, B7:

A possible guitar melody to fit with this sequence could be:

This uses the chord sequence as the basis for a melody suitable for a lead guitar, decorating the chord notes to produce a flowing line. This could become the main melody, varying rhythm and texture, and perhaps adding in some parts for strings and brass to provide more variety.

With varied repetitions, the structure is starting to evolve. The version you hear on the CD follows this outline:

C *A pop-style group*

- There is an introduction consisting of two 4-bar phrases.
- This texture continues, accompanying the opening guitar melody and its extension into a further 2-bar phrase using Am, Em, F and E, heard twice, before B7 leads to a slightly decorated restatement of the main melody.
- This new pattern is repeated without the guitar and with a different drum beat helping to vary the texture. It leads to another new pattern (Am, C, Am and B7) with the accompanying instruments joined by a trumpet.
- This leads in turn to a repeat of the main melodic ideas from the beginning.

- The linking passage returns with a fuller orchestration, enriching the texture, before the final statement of four bars of the melody and the outro or rounding-off passage.

Summary of structure: intro – verse – linking passage/bridge – verse – linking passage/bridge – verse (part) – outro

The wind ensemble

This could be just a group of one instrumental type – for example saxophones, flutes or clarinets – or a mixed ensemble, for example a woodwind quartet of flute, oboe, clarinet and bassoon, or a wind quintet of flute, oboe, clarinet, French horn and bassoon. We decided to work with a wind ensemble, including French horn.

We chose a main melody or motif and created ideas on how it could be accompanied. Here is the main melodic idea:

E *Wind ensemble*

D

Listening activity

Listen to realisations (created through Sibelius software) of these pieces on CD tracks 39–40.

In the first example, the tonality is mostly A minor: is this a problem? Should it change? If so, which keys are possible and where might the changes occur?

The structure is based on the opening sequence plus a further progression of Am Em F E and a closing pattern introducing the chord of C: how are repetitions of the melody varied? How are the 'verses' linked? How is the piece brought to a close?

In the second example, the structure, texture and melodies are much more complex: follow the outline given below and try to identify all the elements:

- The introduction is based on five notes of the main motif, and then establishes a rhythmic accompaniment in 7/8 time.
- The main idea of eight bars is presented initially by the flute and restated imitatively by oboe and bassoon, in major key.
- A linking passage based on the semiquaver phrase from the first bar of the melody is passed through the instruments.
- The melody is shared firstly by flute and clarinet and then by oboe and flute in a minor key.
- A further linking passage is based on the opening pattern of five notes.
- The main melody and accompaniment are now adapted to the whole tone scale by ensuring that every interval is a whole tone, rather than a mixture of tones and semitones as before.
- The final section consists of overlapping entries in the woodwind instruments, with the horn playing the main melody in augmentation (double note values).

Remember

As well as researching the range and characteristics of each instrument in the group you choose, you would need, hopefully, to be able to access players who could offer advice on the suitability of the music for the instruments even if they will not ultimately be able to play it.

Further study

In this chapter we have looked at the different elements which make up the Areas of Study (AoS) and the three strands which will form part of your composition for Unit 2. We have also looked at ways of combining the different elements of music and developing them into specific compositions. Finally, we looked at the various ways of notating your music and the positive and negative features of the different approaches.

It is worth restating at this point the importance of an understanding of staff notation, the international language of music. It is emphasised not only because of its precision but because it will open routes to such a wide range of musical possibilities for any music student at whatever different level and in whatever different style or genre.

◼ Suggestions for practice compositions

Before you write your final compositions for the exam it is worth writing as many practice pieces as you can. Here are some suggestions for combinations to try.

Unit 2 (Composing and Appraising)

1   Combining AoS1 (rhythm and metre) and AoS4 (timbre and dynamics), compose a piece of music linked to the world music strand. You may use Caribbean, African or Indian music as your influence, and your composition should either be based on a clear structure built around a range of ostinato patterns or should combine a variety of rhythmic patterns with strong chord progressions.

2   Combining AoS2 (harmony and tonality) and AoS5 (structure and form), compose a piece of music linked to the popular music of the 20th and 21st centuries strand. Your composition should include either a vocal part or a part for a solo instrument.

Unit 4 (Composing)

1   Using AoS3 (texture and melody) and AoS4 (timbre and dynamics), compose a piece of music in rondo form for (a) tuned and untuned percussion, (b) a small group of string instruments, or (c) a group of instrumentalists drawn from your GCSE music group.

2   Using AoS1 (rhythm and metre) and AoS2 (harmony and tonality), write a piece of music in ternary form which contrasts either (a) metre or (b) tonality or (c) both. You should use at least two instruments, one capable of playing chords and one melody instrument.

■ Suggestions for further study

Listening possibilities are virtually endless: you can choose any piece of music and use it to explore how the composer has used the various different elements of music. There is a list of suggested pieces to listen to on page 179, although you shouldn't limit yourself to just this list – choose as wide a range of music as possible (your teacher can make other suggestions for you).

Your own interests will lead you to listen to particular styles of music, but while following this course you must make sure that you listen to as much music as possible, exploring areas you have not ventured into as yet. There are many exciting and rewarding pieces of music just waiting to be discovered.

You could aim to widen your listening by tuning in to a range of radio stations: local radio, Radio 1, Radio 2, Radio 3, Classic FM and so on.

If you have ready access to the internet, you could download tracks from a wide range of music sites, covering different styles and genres, particularly those with which you are unfamiliar.

When you watch films, as well as watching the action, notice how the music helps create the atmosphere. Ask yourself how this is done.

Take part in as much music making as possible, across as wide a range as possible: variety of musical experience is essential as you learn composing skills.

Chapter summary

7

In this chapter you have learnt:

✔ details on each AoS

✔ different ways of combining elements to produce a composition

✔ suggestions for ways to start a composition based on the elements of music

✔ about using different combinations of instruments and voices

✔ the ways in which ICT can be used within composition

✔ about choosing what type of composition to write

✔ about the use of notation and the requirements of the examination

✔ about the various types of notation that are acceptable

✔ about which form of notation to use

✔ suggestions for improving listening skills

✔ suggestions for practice compositions

✔ suggestions for further study.

Revision quiz

1. Give a brief description of the meaning of each of the elements covered by the five AoS.

2. Explain the difference between simple and compound time.

3. What is a *syncopated* rhythm?

4. What is the difference between diatonic and chromatic music?

5. Name the four cadences and explain the differences between them.

6. What is a *tierce de Picardie*?

7. Explain the difference between major, minor and modal.

8. Give the order in which sharps and flats are added.

9. What is the difference between a harmonic/ homophonic texture and a contrapuntal/ polyphonic one?

10. What is the difference between a conjunct melody and a disjunct one?

11. Which family of instruments can use **all** of these techniques: con arco/with a bow, *pizzicato*/ plucked, double-stopping and *tremolo*/ *tremolando*?

12. Place these dynamics in the correct order from quietest to loudest: *f pp mf p ff mp*

13. Using the letters A B and so on, show a plan for each of the following structures/forms: binary, ternary, rondo, arch-form.

14. What is a ground bass?

15. What is the difference between a strophic and a through-composed song?

8 Choosing the area of composition

Objectives

In this chapter you will learn:

what you should consider for your composition

about the requirements of the examination

how to link to the Strands of Learning

how to combine instruments and/or voices for your composition

how to develop ideas.

■ Introduction

This chapter will focus on composing activities based on the individual Areas of Study as starting points. It will explain the examination requirements and offer advice on linking compositions to different styles, genres and strands. It will offer suggestions for developing musical ideas and will look at the process of deciding on the actual resources – vocal, instrumental, ICT – for your composition.

■ The examination requirements

There are two composition units: Unit 2 (Composing and Appraising Music) and Unit 4 (Composing Music). For more information on these, you can refer back to Chapter 1 on page 9 and Chapter 6 on pages 90–91. For each unit, you have to combine at least two different AoS from the five available. For Unit 2, you have to link your composition to one of the three Strands of Learning. The examination board will choose which one is used each year.

There have already been suggestions in chapter 7 on pages 106–107 and page 112 as to how the AoS might be combined but the final decision is yours. Each combination of two AoS opens up a wide range of possible compositions and, for Unit 2, a variety of links to a particular strand.

Activity

Work out all the possible combinations of two different AoS (there are ten).

Each of these possible combinations can be linked to any of the styles and genres within a particular strand for Unit 2 while, for Unit 4, you can choose any style or genre you want. It is easy to see, therefore, that the choice you will have for your compositions is extremely wide and varied.

■ Further examples of combinations of AoS

Combining AoS2 (harmony and tonality) with AoS5 (structure and form) could result in the following type of composition:

A composition in ternary form where the first section (A) is in a major key with a melody which is mainly diatonic but includes some chromatic decoration, harmonised by a mixture of **primary** and **secondary chords** with, perhaps, some use of **added sevenths**. It might include some modulation. The second section (B) might be written over a pedal or drone and have a more modal feel. The first section (A) would be restated (perhaps with some variation of melody and/or harmony). An introduction and/or **coda** could be added.

Your choice of AoS will lead to decisions as to the resources to be used.

Objectives

You will learn:

about the examination requirements

what you should consider when you are choosing the combination of AoS

what to consider when deciding on the vocal and/or instrumental resources to use

which genre or style might be appropriate.

Key terms

Primary chords: chords based on the first, fourth and fifth notes of the scale; thus, in C major, chords/triads built on C, F and G.

Secondary chords: chords based on the second, third and sixth notes of the scale; in C major, these would be the D minor, E minor and A minor triads.

Added seventh: adding a further note on top of the normal triad: a seventh added to chords of C and F produces a major seventh chord; added to the chord of G it produces a dominant seventh; added to chords of Dm, Em and Am it results in a minor seventh chord.

Coda: a rounding-off section.

Here are some examples:

- To use AoS2 will require two or more pitched instruments or a keyboard capable of producing harmonies and establishing a key.

- Choosing AoS3 means you have to have a pitched instrument to play a melody, and either several instruments or one capable of producing different textures.

- AoS4 will require different instruments to show a range of timbre; your chosen instruments or resources must be capable of varying the dynamics.

- Combining two of AoS1, AoS4 and AoS5 means you can use unpitched percussion, but combining any one of these with AoS2 or AoS3 will require pitched instruments.

AQA *Examiner's tip*

Choose your combinations of AoS carefully. Work on several short pieces to try out different combinations before you make your final decision.

■ Practical activities

AoS1 (rhythm and metre)

- Choose a time signature.
- Compose five different rhythms.
- Introduce them on different instruments (pitched and/or unpitched), producing a layered composition.

AoS2 (harmony and tonality)

- Choose a key (major or minor).
- Write a short chord progression using four to six chords (you can repeat one or more of them within the sequence).
- Choose an accompanying instrument to play these chords.
- Work out a suitable pattern of notes for the chords, such as an Alberti-style accompaniment, spread chords, a waltz style, and so on. An Alberti bass can be a good way of presenting a chordal accompaniment on piano. This chord sequence:

A

…translates into this Alberti-style accompaniment:

B

AoS3 (texture and melody)

- Starting with a single line, bring in further tuned and/or untuned instruments to vary the texture.
- Establish the texture.
- Add a melody on an instrument/voice of your choice.

AoS4 (timbre and dynamics)

- Choose two or more different instruments, tuned or untuned.
- Write two or four short phrases using a question and answer pattern.
- Vary the dynamics either by contrast or by gradual increase/decrease.

AoS5 (structure and form)

- Choose any of the forms listed within this AoS (see pages 36–41).
- Make decisions as to instrumentation.
- Compose the first section.

■ Incorporating specific styles/genres

Remember that your choice of resources will influence the range of styles/genres which are possible.

AoS1 (rhythm and metre)

You could choose orchestral percussion to link to the Western Classical tradition; using a drum kit or electronically produced sounds would fit the 'popular music of the 20th and 21st centuries' strand; world music instrumentation would provide a number of different starting points.

AoS2 (harmony and tonality)

For the Western Classical tradition, you might choose to compose for voices or for a small ensemble of orchestral instruments, using traditional diatonic harmonies; similarly, electric guitars and synthesisers could use these harmonies, perhaps with the harmonic patterns characteristic of the blues; world music voices and/or instruments might point to the composition of a calypso, a raga, a piece of reggae music, or a call-and-response style piece, perhaps using some of the modes or scales found in these styles.

AoS3 (texture and melody)

A wide variety of textural opportunities exist within the styles available in each strand, and your melody would need to be appropriate. For example, your composition could be based on the principle of the concerto, with its element of contrast, which would link it to the Western Classical tradition.

AoS4 (timbre and dynamics)

Choice of instruments will very much determine the strand, but the style/genre might showcase the sounds of a particular orchestral instrument, or be atmospheric music for a film (popular music of the 20th and 21st centuries), or showcase a specific world music instrument or ensemble, such as a group of African percussion instruments.

AoS5 (structure and form)

You might choose, for example, to use an established form and traditional harmony, the 12-bar blues or an Indian raga as your starting point.

Activity

Listen to possible openings for these pieces on the CD:

AoS1 on track 41
AoS2 on track 42
AoS3 on track 43
AoS4 on track 44

Try to decide what style is used.

Identify the link to a strand.

Writing more

Practical activities

Having worked on an opening for a composition, you now need to think about how to extend and develop your piece. What follows is not an exhaustive list, rather some suggestions for each of the starts made in response to the outlines given in the previous chapter.

AoS1 (rhythm and metre)

The first example on the CD uses a mixture of tuned and untuned percussion and introduces five different rhythms. Here are some ways these ideas could be developed:

- Alter the rhythms so that each has fewer or more beats in the pattern, such as 3/4, 7/8 or 5/4.
- Introduce a time shift by concentrating on one of the rhythms and taking away or adding beats.
- Alter some of the rhythms so that you produce a **polyrhythmic** composition.

AoS2 (harmony and tonality)

This composition started with a simple bass guitar rhythm and chords strummed on an acoustic guitar. The opening chord progression (Em C Am Em B⁷ C Am B⁷) and the key of E minor have been established. Here are some ways of extending this piece:

- Introduce a melodic line (on electric/lead guitar) above a repeat of the chord progression.
- Treating this 6-bar melody as a 'question', balance it with an 'answer'.
- Modulate.
- Introduce additional chord progressions to extend the range of chords/harmony used.

AoS3 (texture and melody)

Look at the melody which has already featured in Chapter 6 (see page 92) and Chapter 7 (see page 100). The composition based on this melody opens with a simple broken chord pattern on piano, which is extended in similar style to accompany the first four bars of the melody. There are a number of different ideas for the next step:

- Basing the composition on the melody given in Chapter 7 on page 100, the piano accompaniment could be continued in the same style.
- The texture could be altered by altering the piano style to that of an Alberti bass pattern.
- The accompaniment could become sustained chords.
- The melody could move to the piano while the flute adds a countermelody.

Objectives

You will learn:

about practical activities for continuing each composition begun in the previous chapter

about general suggestions for developing compositions.

Key terms

Polyrhythm: where several different rhythms are used together.

A

AoS4 (timbre and dynamics)

Initially an acoustic guitar and clarinet were chosen for this example. Contrasts of timbre and dynamics are exploited early on by the drop from f (*forte* or loud) to p (*piano* or quiet), before a slight increase for the entry of the melody line. Here are some ideas for extending this further:

B

- The tone of the clarinet varies a lot across its range (the low notes sound quite different from the higher notes). By making the clarinet line use the whole of the instrument's range, you can bring different timbres into the composition.
- Full chords on the guitar can be contrasted with a lighter, finger-picked style.
- The clarinet could take on an accompanying role while the guitar demonstrates its full range or concentrates on one particular area.
- Introducing additional instruments will bring in new timbres.

AoS5 (structure and form)

The given opening for this (see page 133) is planned as the returning feature within a rondo form. Strictly speaking, in rondo form the main section (A) returns without alteration each time. However, you could vary the main section each time it returns, as long as the basic outline is recognisable. These ideas could be used to develop this structure:

- composing contrasting sections (episodes)
- featuring different instruments from the quartet within these episodes
- varying the first section on its returns
- modulating
- adding an introduction and/or coda.

Activity

Listen to the extended versions of these pieces on the CD:

AoS1 on track 46
AoS2 on track 47
AoS3 on track 48
AoS4 on track 49
AoS5 on track 50

Make notes on how the pieces have been extended.

What else could be done?

Decide what you would do.

In this chapter you have learnt:

✔ about the examination requirements for composing

✔ about how to combine two or more elements to produce a composition

✔ about suggestions for ways to start a composition based on each of the elements of music

✔ about suggestions for developing these openings

✔ about linking compositions to the strands.

Revision quiz

1 What is the minimum number of AoS which you must combine in your compositions?

2 How many possible combinations of two different AoS are there?

3 Who will decide which strand is used as the link for the Unit 2 composition each year?

4 Does each strand have only one style or genre in it?

5 Name three different forms which can be used in AoS5.

6 What are the three types of tonality, each beginning with 'm'?

7 Explain the difference between a primary chord and a secondary chord.

8 Explain the differences between a major seventh, a minor seventh and a dominant seventh.

9 What is a 'coda'?

10 Give five examples of pitched percussion and five examples of unpitched percussion.

11 Name two instruments which can provide different textures on their own.

12 Explain what is meant by a 'layered composition'.

13 What is meant by an Alberti-style accompaniment?

14 Explain what is meant by using 'question and answer phrases'.

15 Name the four AoS where your choice of instrumental and/or vocal resources will strongly determine the strand.

16 What is *polyrhythm*?

17 What happens to the music if it modulates?

18 What are the advantages of using modulation in a composition based on tonality?

19 What is a *countermelody*?

20 Within *rondo* form, what is the function of an episode?

Objectives

In this chapter you will learn:

about the appraisal for Unit 2 (Composing and Appraising Music)

how to approach appraisal

how to prepare your answers

how to make sure you have responded well.

■ Introduction

This chapter will deal with the appraisal part of Unit 2 (Composing and Appraising). It will:

- look at the way the Appraisal Booklet will be set out
- examine each of the questions in detail
- explain what is expected within your answer
- offer advice on how to plan your writing
- suggest ways of organising your presentation
- explain the way in which it will be marked
- offer advice as to how to gain the top marks.

9.1 The appraisal

The appraisal deals with six different areas, and will remain the same whichever strand is set by the examination board. Six questions will appear on the inside cover of the Appraisal Booklet, and you will use these as a framework for your appraisal, which is to be written within the booklet. However, you are allowed to set out your answers on separate paper as long as you make sure that you have addressed all six bullet points.

The six questions will be:

- What Areas of Study did you choose, and what is the focus of your composition within the given strand?
- Why did you choose these Areas of Study and the particular focus within the given strand?
- How did you go about composing your music and how was the final recording achieved?
- What difficulties did you encounter during the task and how did you overcome them?
- What makes your composition successful in relation to the chosen Areas of Study and focus within the given strand?
- What is the relationship of your composition to its context?

The examination requirements

In this unit, the appraisal is worth 10 per cent of your final GCSE marks, the same as the composition you are appraising. You will have up to two hours of controlled time in which to write the appraisal. You will do this alone, and the time you spend will be fully supervised.

Obviously, you will be able to prepare your answers in advance, and will be able to take your notes into the room with you when you write the appraisal.

A *You need to prepare for your appraisal*

The assessment criteria

Your appraisal will be marked out of 20. These 20 marks are divided into four bands of five marks. A mark of 0 can be awarded if your work is judged to show no evidence at all of the skills required.

To gain a mark in the top band (20–16), your appraisal must show:

- a thorough understanding of how well your composition has worked in terms of the areas of study and strand chosen
- a detailed and accurate description of the composing process and a sound understanding of how you developed your musical ideas
- acknowledgement of any problems and difficulties you met and a clear description of the steps you took to solve them
- identification of any weaknesses in your music
- a thorough knowledge of the chosen musical elements and of the characteristics and conventions of the strand chosen
- a wide range of relevant musical vocabulary
- a firm grasp of spelling, grammar and punctuation.

This is what is expected for the highest marks. Of course, if you do less well on the various points you will receive fewer marks until, in the lowest mark band (5–1), your answers will be considered to have limited value (or none), and your written work will contain so many errors that an examiner will find it difficult to follow the comments you are making.

You should, of course, aim to achieve high marks: to set your sights lower risks the loss of many marks.

AQA *Examiner's tip*

Prepare your responses well in advance by making notes in your composer's notebook as you develop your composition and record it.

How to prepare and plan

■ Methods and strategies

Keep a list of what you will have to cover in your appraisal with you as you compose. Refer to it at regular intervals and make notes under the different headings as the work progresses.

One of the first matters you will be able to cover will be the choice of areas of study: you should make notes as to which two (or more) AoS you have chosen and why – bullet points will be fine at this stage. Remember that this is to justify your choice in terms of your composition, so your reasoning must be logical and worthwhile.

For example, if you were to write:

> I chose AoS4 (Timbre and Dynamics) and AoS5 (Structure and Form) because I thought it would be really easy to do this on Sibelius by choosing different instruments, contrasting the dynamics and using a form such as ternary or rondo.

… this would be seen as a low value response, as it seems to reflect little real thought and be aiming for the simplest possible solution.

If, on the other hand, your answer was more along these lines:

> After careful thought and following close consideration of the available resources and my own experiences and strengths as a composer and performer, I decided to combine AoS2 (Harmony and Tonality) and AoS5 (Structure and Form). My main reasons for choosing these are:
>
> I would be able to write a piece of music for the piano, the instrument I play and understand well.
>
> I would be able to use major and minor keys to establish different moods.
>
> I would be able to use a wide range of chords, reflecting the fact that I like to experiment with different chords at the piano.
>
> I would be able to use a form such as rondo form, which would allow me to contrast different keys, moods and ways of writing for the piano.

Objectives

You will learn:

how to approach the preparation for your appraisal

about different strategies for setting out your answers.

… this would be seen as a well-thought-out response, justifying and explaining the reasons for your choices in detail.

Keep a detailed log of the process of composition. It would be a good idea to get into the habit of doing this as you work on your practice compositions, detailing what features of a particular AoS or combination of AoS you are using and how you have used them.

When you come across problems, make a note of them. However, make sure that you don't keep repeating similar comments at different points of your final appraisal: after preparation, you will be able to group together similar problems and give explanations of how you overcame them and were able to make progress. Your final appraisal is to be written within the Appraisal Booklet or can be word processed. Your response must be written in continuous prose, and part of your assessment will be based on your ability to write clearly and accurately, using specialist musical vocabulary where appropriate.

This process of keeping a log and noting down difficulties and solutions applies equally to the matter of making the final recording of your composition, whether through acoustic means, by technology or by a combination of both. Make sure that you check carefully the range of the instruments and voices you are going to use. If you have particular performers in mind, find out exactly how good they are and the range of notes they can play or sing comfortably. If you are going to use sounds generated by software, and intend to go beyond the normal range of notes available on an equivalent acoustic instrument, make sure that you state within your submission that you are composing for computer-generated sounds, and alter instrument names on the score, for instance from 'Flute' to 'Flute sound'.

Writing and reviewing answers

Two responses were given on page 140 as examples of writing about the reasons behind your choice of two AoS for your composition. At that point, it was explained that the second one showed evidence of careful thought and logical reasoning behind the choice, and was therefore the better answer.

Objectives

You will learn:

about writing and reviewing answers in preparation for the appraisal.

Activity

Consider the two responses below to a description of the process of starting a composition for a piece combining AoS2 (harmony and tonality) with AoS3 (texture and melody).

Discuss each of them with someone else in your group and decide which is the better answer and why. Pool your findings with the rest of the students and your teacher, and come to conclusions.

I decided to start by making up a tune and picked out some notes on the keyboard until I came up with some that sounded OK. I then wanted to add some chords to them so I took each note in turn and played other notes with it until I found some that fitted. Using Sibelius, I chose a violin for the tune and put the chords onto a piano. I then played them back and changed any that didn't sound right.

Before I started work on the actual composition, I took some time to decide which instruments I was going to use: this was important because I had to be able to add harmony and be able to vary the texture. I can play the piano and my best friend has got Grade 5 on the flute so I thought I would start with these two instruments.

The next decision I had to make was about the key to use. As I wanted to write a happy piece, I decided on a major key and, after talking to my friend, the key of D major was chosen for the tonic key, as we were both confident of being able to play music in this key. It is important to start music for these AoS by making the key obvious, so I decided to use the chords of D, G and A in the opening phrase, played just by the piano as an introduction. I used them to form a strong progression ending on A, the dominant.

Finally, with these chords in mind, I sat at the piano and gradually worked out question and answer phrases for flute with piano accompaniment.

AQA Examiner's tip

Let your teacher see your written responses. Take careful note of the feedback you are given.

As you work through your composition and prepare it for the final recording, you will have kept detailed notes. At various points during the early part of this course, where you are composing short practice pieces, you should try to write answers for the different parts of the appraisal.

Here are other practice tasks and questions for you to try during the course as you work on different pieces. (You need not do them all for each piece.)

1   Give full details of the AoS chosen, and the strand, with particular attention to the style/genre you have chosen from within that strand, for example film music from 'popular music of the 20th and 21st centuries'.

2   Give full details of how the final recording was achieved, including steps taken to make sure that the balance was good, that all performers were happy with their music, that the required rehearsals had taken place, and how many times the piece was recorded before you were satisfied with the result.

3   What were the difficulties you encountered during your work on this composition, and what did you do to solve them?

4   How is your composition successful in terms of the chosen AoS and the focus you have chosen within the strand?

5   How does your composition fit the context of the music chosen? For the film music example, this might involve explaining the genre of film and/or the particular situation, the event and/or the character, and explaining how your music is appropriate.

A *Seek feedback from your teacher on your answers*

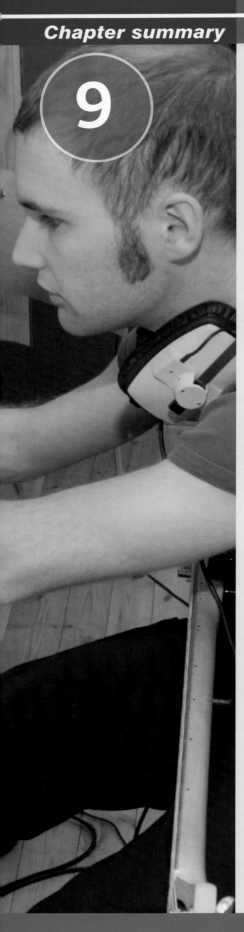

In this chapter you have learnt:

✔ what will be expected in the appraisal for Unit 2 (Composing and Appraising Music), and what you will have to cover in the course of your appraisal

✔ how to approach the appraisal and prepare your answers

✔ how to make sure you have responded well

✔ about the examination requirements

✔ about the assessment criteria

✔ different strategies for setting out your answers

✔ about writing and reviewing answers in preparation for the appraisal.

Revision quiz

1. The questions for the appraisal will appear on the inside cover of the Appraisal Booklet: only answers written in this booklet will be marked. True or false?

2. Can you choose which questions to answer?

3. Who decides which strand to use – you or the examination board?

4. If the examination board has chosen the strand, how can you write about why *you* chose it?

5. Why should it be possible to gain a high mark in the appraisal?

6. On page 139 of this chapter, seven areas to aim for to gain a mark in the top band (20–16) were listed: write down as many as you can remember before going back to check what you have missed.

7. What are the five headings you should put at the top of separate pages as you work on your compositions? List as many as you can remember and then check what you missed.

8. If you are using computer-generated sounds and want to use notes that an instrument on your score cannot play (such as the G below Middle C on a flute), what should you do when you submit your composition and score?

9. How many styles/genres can you remember from each strand? Try to name three from each (the strands are the Western Classical tradition, Popular music of the 20th and 21st centuries, and World music).

10. How much controlled time will you have for writing your final appraisal?

Objectives

In this chapter you will learn:

how to prepare for the examination

how to make the best use of controlled or supervised time

how to complete your submission with the necessary documents and recording.

Introduction

It is important that you are fully prepared to use the time you have available for the final composition and the appraisal. All are done under supervised time, meaning that the hours available will be logged while supervised in a work area. For the compositions, you will have 20 hours for Unit 2, 25 for Unit 4. For the appraisal, you will have up to two hours. You will be able to use instruments, computers and word processors. You will be able to develop compositional ideas between sessions but your teacher must be able to verify that all work submitted is your own. Although you will be able to prepare your appraisal in advance, all final written work must remain behind in a secure place.

Supervised time and controlled assessment

Your compositions for Units 2 and 4 are done under supervision within a designated work area. For Unit 2, you will have 20 hours, for Unit 4, 25 hours. Although most of your work will be done within this area, it will be possible to develop your ideas between your composing sessions. However, it is very important that your teacher will be able to say with certainty that all the work is yours: if not, you must declare any specific help you received from others. You will, therefore, be able to make good use of your time within the work area and, in between, be able to plan the next stage of your composition ready for the next time. You will be able to refer to books and notes as well as ask your teacher about a matter of fact or a technique but, of course, your teacher cannot comment directly on the progress of your work in a specific way unless you then note this on your *Candidate Record Form*.

Your appraisal will be written during up to two further hours in a work area. You will not be able to take your written appraisal, whether completed or not, out of the work area.

Strategies before the start of the controlled time

As you learn about the different AoS and how to use the various elements of music, you should gradually be deciding exactly which AoS to combine. The examination board will announce the strand at the beginning of your GCSE course and, as you learn new ways to compose, you should look at different ways in which you can link your music into the strand and write short compositions linked to a range of styles or genres within it.

Your school will decide how long each composing session will be: you need to prepare by getting used to spending longer periods composing, making constructive use of 45 minutes, an hour, two hours and so on.

Preparation for your appraisal can be done outside the controlled area, and you can take written notes into the sessions with you. As two hours are allowed for this, it is likely to be completed in one session, two at the most.

Before the controlled time starts, you will have been told which strand has been selected. You should have time to do a practice piece, combining the two (or more) AoS you chose with a particular style/genre from the given strand. You will already have gained a lot of ideas and learnt a lot of techniques: use them sensibly, carefully planning your music to demonstrate your understanding of the AoS, the strand and the musical aspects (refer to Chapter 6 page 92). Make a recording of at least part of this practice composition and write an appraisal, if only in note form.

Objectives

You will learn:

the meaning of 'supervised time' or 'controlled time'

the rules and examination requirements as applied to supervised or controlled time

strategies to use before starting your composing or appraising time

how to use your time wisely.

Remember

Your final composition is written without any help.

It is very important that you can write down your musical ideas accurately: you will be returning to them in different sessions to continue work and must be able to tell exactly what you have done. Taking time to work confidently with notation is very important.

Practice pieces

Make sure you know the range of musical elements within each AoS you will use, and that your composition will enable you to demonstrate your understanding of them.

Practise composing using the resources you intend to use for your final piece, so that you can hear them performed and learn more about techniques, the use of instruments and equipment and how to achieve a good balance.

Try to complete at least one short piece for each strand, so that any problems can be discussed and resolved. Your ability to compose will improve with practice.

How to use your time wisely

Having started your final composition, you will want to revise and re-write sections of it. Never delete discarded material at this stage: keep it safe in case you find it useful at a later stage.

As you progress, you will probably find that you get stuck: leave that passage and move on to another. If there is still much to be done, don't spend too much time trying to make one short section perfect – better to get the whole composition sketched out.

If a session was fairly disappointing in terms of progress, don't get disillusioned: a poor session is often followed by a more productive one as you return to the work refreshed.

At all costs, try to avoid abandoning a composition part way through and completely restarting: your controlled time does not begin again.

> **AQA** *Examiner's tip*
>
> Remember to allow time within your 20 hours to check your score for accuracy. Edit it carefully to show – as appropriate – articulation, dynamics, phrasing and underlay of the text.

Making the best recording

Although your composition is marked for its responses to the chosen AoS, the strand and the musical aspects, you should aim to produce a recording that clearly demonstrates your detailed, final intentions.

As you work on practice pieces, and have finalised the line-up of resources you will be using, make some practice recordings: this might take some time, so be sure that everyone can come and work at this. You will probably have to experiment with microphones, with microphone placement and with balance. Wherever possible use a multi-track recorder, with each instrument playing into a separate microphone: this will help you achieve a better final mix as you will be able to control levels and panning more easily.

If you intend to realise your composition via technology, it is very important that you pay close attention to performing and expressive detail – dynamics, articulation, balance, tempo and so on. On most software packages, simply setting an overall dynamic level – *f* for example – is rarely satisfactory: different instruments play at different levels, and, with software such as Sibelius, a single piano or guitar note is quieter than a chord, even if the dynamic is unchanged. These are all things you must think about.

Similarly, when shading dynamics, acoustic performers do this much better than software: whether you are using Cubase, Logic, Guitar-Pro, Sibelius or another program, the difference between **mp** and **mf** is barely noticeable, and you will have to make a separate 'performance' file so that all the contrasts and details you want are heard.

Presenting the musical score

Look back at the different types of notation described in Chapter 7 (pages 114–21). Your final presentation must include enough detail to enable the examiner to understand exactly what your intentions are in your composition. This is why the use of staff notation is so important, as it is such a precise form of presenting music; it is the most concise way of getting across a lot of information. Of course, this will depend on the style of music you are composing, and you should use the notation method that is most appropriate (for guitar music, for example, this might be tab).

Consider these bars from Debussy's 'La fille aux cheveux de lin':

A

Objectives

You will learn:

how to make the best recording

how to present the final musical score

how to complete the Candidate Record Form.

Remember

The recording must be on a CD or mini-disc, playable on standard equipment. You must not submit your music as an MP3 file, a WAV file, in mini-disc long-play mode or on a CD which can be played only through a computer. If you are in any doubt, check with your teacher in good time: the recording is sent off with the rest of your work to an examiner who will want to listen to your music as he or she follows your score.

- Style: *Très calme et doucement expressif* and *sans rigueur*.
- Tempo: $\downarrow$ = 66 (i.e. 66 bpm).
- Dynamic: ***p*** .
- Phrasing, articulation and the entry of the left hand are also shown clearly.
- The instrument is identified.

Key terms

Très calme et doucement expressif: very calm and sweetly expressive.

Sans rigueur: without strictness, i.e. play flexibly, or with rubato.

bpm: beats per minute.

Activity

Try presenting this music as a graphic score, in tab or through an annotation: each will take longer and be less precise.

Did you know ??????

The recording can be made after the controlled time if no changes are made to the composition.

If you are using a different method, make sure you include, where appropriate:

- information about melodic and rhythmic ideas
- a description of the structure and development of your piece
- a plan of keys and chords used
- information on texture, timbre, dynamics, articulation
- lyrics
- full information on how any electronic sound sources were used and processed.

Completing the Candidate Record Form

This form will include your name, candidate number, centre name and number, the title of your composition, and the track of the CD/mini-disc on which it can be found (if your teacher is submitting everyone's compositions together on one disc). You will also be asked for information as to the Areas of Study chosen and the focus wthin the strand.

Make sure all information is accurate and that you sign the declaration, confirming it to be all your own work. Your teacher also has to sign to say that the work is yours.

Centre Number		Candidate Number		For Examiner's use
Surname			
Other Names			
Candidate Signature			

⬜ ⬜ | General Certificate of Secondary Education June 2010

Music　　　　　　　　　**42702/AB**

Appraisal Booklet for Unit 2: Composing and Appraising Music

You may use:
- your final version of the score and/or annotation of your composition
- any notes you have made during the process of composing and preparing the final completed recording.

Time allowed
- Up to 2 hours

Areas of Study ....
....

Instructions
- You will have up to 2 hours of Controlled Time in which to write your appraisal. It may be hand-written on the lined pages of this booklet or be word-processed on separate sheets to be attached to the booklet.
- Use black ink or black ball-point pen if your appraisal is hand-written.
- Work in this booklet must be your own.
- This Appraisal Booklet must **not** be removed from your centre.

Information
- There are 20 marks for the Composition and 20 marks for the Appraisal
- The questions on page 2 of this booklet should be used to help you structure your appraisal of your work.
- You can use any notes made during the process of composing and preparing the final completed recording.
- It is not expected that you need to write more than can be contained in this booklet.
- Your appraisal should be written in continuous prose. In your appraisal, you will be marked on your ability to:
  - use good English
  - organise information clearly
  - use specialist vocabulary where appropriate.

42702/AB

B *Your appraisal booklet may look something like this*

In this chapter you have learnt:

✔ about supervised or controlled time

✔ about the implications of supervised/controlled time

✔ how to prepare for the examination

✔ about strategies to use before starting your composing or appraising time

✔ how to manage your time

✔ how to prepare the final recording

✔ about the presentation of the musical score

✔ how to complete your Candidate Record Form.

Revision quiz

Answer the following as true or false:

1. *Supervised* or *controlled time* means that you are in charge of the time you spend on your composition and appraisal.

2. You have 20 hours to complete your composition for Unit 2.

3. You have 20 hours to write your appraisal.

4. You will be able to prepare your composition and appraisal in advance and bring your ideas into the supervised sessions.

5. You have to do the composition in four sessions of five hours each.

6. You must complete the appraisal within one session.

7. The quality of the final recording of your composition is assessed as part of this unit.

8. It is easy to get good dynamic contrast on ICT by simply setting all the individual volumes to the same level.

9. You will be able to ask for help with your composition during a supervised session if you find you just can't think what to do next.

10. You should try to use staff notation for your musical score because it is detailed and concise.

11. Both you and your teacher must sign the Candidate Record Form.

12. You should allow time within the 20 hours to check your work for detail and accuracy.

11 Making choices

Objectives

In this chapter you will learn:

about the various options available within this Performing Music unit

how to decide which options are best for you

about the requirements of this unit

about the weighting of this unit within the overall examination scheme.

■ Introduction

For Unit 3 (Performing Music), you will perform two different pieces: a solo piece and one where you are a member of a group. This chapter will look at the various options available. Most students take music because they like performing and are good at it. For this reason, this unit carries 40% of your final GCSE mark, more than the Composing or Listening and Appraising units.

Later chapters will deal with developing performing skills, preparing your performance and making your final submission.

This chapter will give information relating to this unit and its place within the examination and will also examine the two solo performance options – acoustic or using technology.

About this component

This unit covers Assessment Objective 1 (AO1) – your performing skills. In it, your ability to perform and/or realise music, demonstrating technical control, expression and interpretation will be marked. You have to perform two different pieces of music: one will be marked as a **solo** performance; in the other, you will take part in a **group** performance. You can, of course, play the same instrument or sing for both of these performances, but you must choose different pieces of music.

Instead of choosing to sing or play acoustically for your solo performance, you might prefer to submit a technology-based performance. This will involve using a sequencer and/or a multi-track recorder. At least three different parts must be inputted and you must perform at least one of them in real or step time. You then use the technology to manipulate the inputted data to achieve a satisfactory performance according to the assessment criteria.

A Audio production session

For the group performance, you will be part of a (usually) small group of players. Your performance can be conducted, and the other performers can be students or not, as seems best for your musical intentions.

Each of your performances is marked out of 30. Remember that, for all acoustic performances, only three of the marks are awarded to reflect the difficulty of the music you play ('Level of Demand'). This means that you must be sure to choose music you can play accurately, confidently and with a strong sense of style.

The top mark for Level of Demand is gained by playing music above the equivalent of Grade 4 standard. If you are not sure what this means, talk to your teacher. If you receive instrumental or singing lessons, you will probably know – but you should still talk to your teacher about the best pieces to choose.

For a technology-based performance, the method of marking is different and falls into five areas:

- accuracy of pitch and rhythm, including evidence of close attention to performing and expressive detail
- care taken to ensure a good balance
- the use of an appropriate dynamic range
- the use of panning to obtain a clear recording and, where necessary, to separate sounds that make use of similar frequency ranges
- evidence of awareness of the style required, including the use of effects such as reverb and delay where appropriate.

As you are being assessed for performing, you must input at least one of the tracks, either in real time or in step time (see page 110).

Take time to choose your pieces. If necessary, work with your teacher to learn or improve the technical skills you need to perform them. If your solo performance is to be accompanied – and it should be if that is how it was written – allow plenty of time to work with your accompanist or get used to the backing track. For your group performance, the group should get together as soon as each member can play his or her part accurately.

For a technology-based performance, make short practice recordings, trying different ways of manipulating the tracks.

In all cases, play to other people to receive feedback and to get used to playing to an audience.

■ Duration

The maximum duration of your performances should be no longer than five minutes. No minimum duration is defined, but you must make sure they are long enough to allow you to demonstrate the skills needed to achieve marks in the top bands. Careful discussion with your teachers and thorough preparation are vital.

B *What will you choose to perform?*

11.2 Choosing an option

The acoustic option

For the solo performance, you will select a piece of music where you will be assessed as an individual. For the acoustic option, this can be one of three types of performance:

- an unaccompanied solo (but only where this is how the music was written)
- an accompanied solo
- a performance of a piece where you will have a substantial solo part within it.

This means that, for the purpose of this examination, you will be playing, singing or maintaining an **independent melodic or rhythmic part** in your chosen piece of music. This includes performances such as **rapping** and **turntablism**.

A A CD mixer

For a solo acoustic performance, the following marks are available:

- level of demand: 3 out of 30
- accuracy: 9 out of 30
- communication: 9 out of 30
- interpretation: 9 out of 30.

Thus, 90% of the marks are for the actual performance of the music, with only 10% to reflect its difficulty. These areas will be explained more fully in the next chapter, but your ability to play your piece well is very important, so much so that it is worth losing a mark for level of demand if it means that you will be able to aim for the top marks in accuracy, communication and interpretation.

It is also possible to accompany yourself as you sing, with the level of demand being assessed **holistically**.

Objectives

You will learn:

what is needed for each of the two solo options.

Key terms

Rapping: speaking rhythmically, using a pattern of rhyming phrases over a musical backing

Turntablism: moving records on turntables and moving the stylus to create music by mixing the sounds. Different turntable techniques include scratching and beat-mixing combined via the mixer.

Holistic: the level of demand of the music performed will be assessed by taking into account the additional complication of performing on two instruments simultaneously (e.g. voice and guitar or voice and piano).

■ The technology-based option

Before you consider the technology-based option, you must make sure that you have access to suitable resources:

- a good quality sequencer such as CubaseSX or Logic Pro 7
- a notation/scoring package such as Sibelius, Coda Finale 2005 or Garageband
- condenser and dynamic microphones (such as those in the Behringer and Edirol ranges)
- a multi-track recorder where you will be able to manipulate the balance of the parts entered, apply panning and, where appropriate, reverb, echo or other effects; a range of models is available from Fostex, Roland, Tascam and others
- possibly a sound processor or an external effects unit (such as those in the Behringer range)
- good-quality headphones from the BOSE, Sennheiser, Sony, Technics or other ranges
- all necessary cabling and connections.

You will be assessed differently for a technology-based performance, with credit given for the quality of your performance in these areas:

- accuracy of pitch and rhythm, including evidence of close attention to performing and expressive detail
- care taken to ensure a good balance
- the use of an appropriate dynamic range
- the use of panning to obtain a clear recording and, where necessary, to separate sounds that use similar frequency ranges
- an awareness of the style required, including the use of effects such as reverb and delay where appropriate.

You will also be expected to give details of the equipment used and of the recording process. Again, these areas will be considered in more detail in the next chapter.

B *Mixing music*

11

In this chapter you have learnt:

✔ about the requirements of Unit 3 (Performing Music)

✔ about Assessment Objective 1 (AO1) Performing skills

✔ about the two different solo performance options

✔ about the main areas of assessment of the solo performance

✔ about some suggestions for equipment needed for a technology-based performance

✔ about some of the technical terms associated with technology-based performances

✔ how to decide between the two solo performance options.

Revision quiz

1 What is assessed in this unit?

2 How many pieces of music will you have to perform?

3 What grade level equivalent will be awarded the top mark for level of demand?

4 Which of the following percentages of the total mark is awarded for the level of demand of your chosen piece?

 a 10% b 15% c 20% d 25% e 30%

5 Of the three other areas of assessment for your solo performance – accuracy, communication and interpretation – which is awarded most marks?

6 What is the minimum number of different parts which must be recorded for a technology-based performance?

7 What is the minimum number of parts **you** must perform in your technology-based piece?

8 What is meant by *panning*?

9 Explain the difference between *real time entry* and *step time entry*.

10 What is meant by a *holistic* assessment?

l learn:

ill need to
s for solo
ces

ill need
sed

nd

t criteria

r
tion.

▮ Introduction

In this chapter, the skills required for the solo and group acoustic performance as well as for technology-based performance will be outlined. Advice will be given on ways of improving your skills in preparation for the examination.

You will also learn more about what you need to do for each option. The range of skills required will be examined and practical activities suggested to enable you to improve and then hone your own skills. A full explanation will be given of the assessment criteria for each option, with details as to what this means in terms of your preparation and final performances.

It is expected that each performance will last no longer than five minutes, though of course it must be long enough to contain sufficient demands to let you access the higher marks.

It is likely that one of the reasons you chose to do music is because you enjoy performing. In this unit you can gain marks for simply doing what you enjoy! As long as you bear a few things in mind, you should approach the final assessment with a real sense of confidence.

It doesn't matter whether you will be playing an instrument or singing. The important aspect of this unit is to choose two pieces of music that you will be able to play really well, and to work on your performance until it matches the areas described in the top bands of marks.

If you have played an instrument or sung for any length of time, you will probably have done various scales or exercises to acquire skills or improve those you have. You might have worked to extend your range if you play a wind instrument or sing, or been introduced to more complex pieces of music. You should always remember to spend time maintaining these skills – daily practice is the best.

If you have had or still receive lessons, you will know some exercises: make sure you work at these on a regular basis – though do vary what you practise to avoid becoming jaded. Check what your playing or singing ability is, bearing in mind that the highest mark for the difficulty of your music will be awarded if it is above the equivalent of Grade 4: if you don't know what this means, talk to your teacher.

◼ Solo performance

Unless the piece you choose was written to be performed by one person, unaccompanied, you will be working with an accompanist as you prepare and then perform your music. Few unaccompanied pieces are really suitable for a GCSE solo performance. Working with an accompanist will help you give a more assured performance with the security that comes from rehearsal and understanding. Your aims are:

- to play accurately
- to communicate the music confidently
- to show real understanding of the style and characteristics of the music.

A *Performing solo*

Objectives

You will learn:

about the skills required for the acoustic options

methods of acquiring and improving skills

strategies for improving performances.

Did you know ??????

A famous concert pianist, Paderewski, once said: 'If I miss one day of practice, I notice it. If I miss two days, the critics notice it. If I miss three days, the audience notices it.'

Group performance

You will also need to play as a member of a (small) group of performers. There must be at least **two live performers**, but a backing track *can* be used as well. It is best to get used to playing with the same people over a long period; in this way, you will all get used to working together, and will understand each other's strengths and weaknesses. If you are already a member of a group such as a flute trio, a string quartet, a rock band, a chamber choir or similar, you will have a basic repertoire of music: talk to your teacher(s) about the difficulty of this music in terms of the examination. Learn your own part and then get together often to make sure you meet the requirements for playing as an **ensemble** (more on this on page 171). This is the extra assessment area for this performance – accuracy, communication and interpretation are still marked.

The element of *togetherness* is the key to a good group performance. Play with a unity of purpose, so that balance, dynamics, intonation and timing are well matched; then if something *does* go wrong during the performance, the rest of the players will have the confidence to carry on until the ensemble is re-established.

Key terms

Ensemble: from the French *ensemble* (meaning 'together'), this can describe any group of people playing or singing together.

Accompanying

It is possible for you to **accompany** another player (or more than one), as this will demonstrate your ability to work with one or more performers, showing responsiveness and rapport. This would count as a **group performance**, not a **solo performance**. Likewise, **duets** are permitted where the two parts are of equal importance, and this too will count as a **group performance**. For example, most piano duets will be acceptable, and there are many pieces of a similar nature written for pairs of instruments.

However, a performance where you are the **soloist** (e.g. a trumpeter accompanied by a piano) will **not count as a group performance** because the accompanist will almost always be accommodating your performance.

Always check your choice with your teacher.

B *Group performance*

Level of Demand

The highest mark is awarded for music above the equivalent to that set at Grade 4 by Rock School, Trinity Guildhall and the Associated Board of the Royal Schools of Music (ABRSM). Music at this level is relatively difficult and you will have to show the ability to deal with a reasonable pitch range, with varying rhythms and dynamics, and, where appropriate, chords and texture.

Accuracy

Here, you will be marked on how securely you are able to play rhythms and pitches. With, for example, the voice and stringed instruments, this will also include intonation. The top band of marks (7–9) is available for:

> *A secure performance in terms of pitch (including intonation, where appropriate) and rhythm. Occasional slips not affecting the fluency of the performance results in a mark at the lower end of this band.*

Obviously, as it is a live performance, the occasional error will not mean you cannot gain a mark in the top band: it is not until the slips and errors affect the flow of the music that your mark will move below this band. Thus, thoroughly learning the music is the first essential.

Communication

For this group of marks, the examiner will be looking at your ability to deliver your music with confidence, to project your performance and to demonstrate your involvement in the music. The top band of marks (7–9) for this will need:

> *A committed, assured, convincing and well-projected performance. The candidate demonstrates a high level of involvement in the music. The music is likely to be complex and demanding.*

Perform your chosen piece with real commitment and a strong sense of assurance, conveying to the audience your sense of conviction. This can come only from real confidence in your own ability to play or sing the music.

Interpretation

You will need to bear in mind the period and style of the music you have chosen to perform. For this section, you will be marked on how well you show an understanding of the characteristics of your chosen piece in terms of period and stylistic conventions. For the top (7–9) band of marks:

Objectives

You will learn:

about the assessment criteria for acoustic performances

about methods of accessing marks in the highest bands

how to prepare for the final performances.

Remember

Both acoustic performances are assessed for accuracy, communication and interpretation. You should always bear in mind what is needed to gain marks in the top band; to aim for a lower mark might result in a really poor effort. The music's Level of Demand is also judged and a mark out of 3 is awarded.

AQA Examiner's tip

Always choose music within your comfort zone: do not play at the limit of (or beyond) your ability as this will increase the pressure during your performance and is more likely to lead to mistakes, costing you marks. What you gain for 'Level of Demand' you will probably lose in the other areas of 'accuracy', 'communication' and 'interpretation'.

> *The candidate shows a mature understanding of both period and style. The tempo is appropriate and mastery of the techniques demanded by the music is evident. The candidate observes the composer's expressive and performance directions. The music is likely to be complex and demanding.*

Stylistic features may include interpretation of dynamics or the playing of ornaments.

Activities

Assessing acoustic performances

1 Listen to a performance by a member of your group, or by a group of performers.

- Assess the performance using the relevant headings: Level of Demand, Accuracy, Communication and Interpretation, and (for group performances) Sense of Ensemble. In all cases, give reasons for your award of marks.
- Discuss your choice of marks with your teacher.

2 Listen to a recording of your own performance, both as an individual and within a group.

- Repeat the assessment and discussion activities.

Group performance

Up to nine marks will be awarded for demonstrating a sense of ensemble – an understanding of how to work closely with others to produce a group performance. For this element, the top band of marks (7–9) are awarded for:

> *A performance showing complete unity of purpose in all aspects of ensemble playing, including balance, timing, intonation and responsiveness to others. If necessary, the candidate shows the ability to react positively to any difficulties which may occur. Marks towards the bottom of this band reflect success in most of these areas.*

Having learned your part, regular practice with the rest of the group will allow you to work at matters of balance, timing, dynamics and responsiveness: make sure you have time to do this. It is vital that the music you choose allows you to demonstrate these skills, playing alongside other performers whose music complements yours in terms of playing melody lines and forming (part of) the accompaniment. Alternatively, as has already been mentioned, if you play piano, guitar or other instrument suitable for accompanying a performer (or more than one), this will be perfectly acceptable.

Remember

In baroque music dynamics are more likely to be tiered than change gradually, and trills are played differently compared with later music:

12.3 Acoustic performance: rapping and turntablism

◼ Rapping

Level of Demand

If you choose to offer this as your acoustic performance, its Level of Demand will be determined by:

- its rhythmic complexity
- the speed of the delivery
- the clarity of the performance and
- how elaborate the final result is.

If you play and rap at the same time, this will gain further credit as part of a holistic assessment.

Accuracy

You will be judged on the fluency of your performance and the extent to which it remains synchronised to its rhythmic backing.

Interpretation

Marks will be gained for clarity of diction and range of dynamics. If you prepare your own backing, this is fine and need not be recorded simultaneously. If you want to be assessed rapping and playing, then these *must be live*, as it is the *live* performance that is assessed.

Do remember that, although the lyrics themselves are not part of the assessment, you must not include any bad, suggestive or offensive language. Should this occur, it will be reported to the examination board as it is not acceptable.

Communication

Marks are awarded for the conviction of your performance, which should demonstrate a sense of commitment and be well projected.

You will need to rehearse your routine so that it can be delivered without hesitation and with the sense of conviction that comes from confidence in your own ability.

Objectives

You will learn:

about the assessment criteria for rapping as part of the acoustic performance option

about the assessment criteria for turntablism as part of the acoustic performance option.

Turntablism

Level of Demand

The Level of Demand will reflect the range of turntable techniques used, including beat juggling, beat mixing, beat matching, and scratching. Scratching can itself be combined with the use of the mixer to produce more elaborate rhythms and patterns, thus increasing the level of demand.

Accuracy

This will be judged through the fluency of the performance and the ability to maintain an underlying pulse.

Interpretation

Marks will be awarded for the smoothness of changes, the clear but seamless merging of beats and the range incorporated into the performance.

Communication

A performance must be convincing, committed and well projected to gain high marks in this category.

You should gradually build up the various skills that you will demonstrate within your performance, and bring them together into a coherent and committed piece that fully exploits the potential of turntables and mixer(s) and achieves a fluent and convincing performance.

A *Turntablist*

12.4 Technology-based performances

Instead of a solo acoustic performance, you may perform using technology. For the purposes of this examination, this involves using a sequencer and/or multi-track recorder. At least three different tracks will be recorded, and then you will manipulate this data to produce a satisfactory performance in terms of the assessment criteria (full details on pages 166–7).

As a minimum, you must perform one of the tracks in either *step time* or *real time* (see page 153). Before you consider doing this option, you must check that you and/or your school have the equipment you will need. These have been referred to on page 155 but some perhaps need a little more explanation:

- a good-quality sequencer such as CubaseSX (Steinberg), Logic Pro 7 or Cakewalk Sonar 7; Roland and Yamaha make a range of keyboards which incorporate sequencers
- a notation/scoring package such as Sibelius, Coda Finale 2005 or Garageband: this is needed because sequencers tend to have limited scoring facilities
- **condenser** and **dynamic microphones** (for example, models by Behringer, Edirol and Shure)
- a multi-track recorder where you will be able to manipulate the balance of the parts entered, apply panning and, where appropriate, reverb, echo or other effects; Fostex, Roland, Tascam and others market a range of models
- possibly a sound processor or external effects unit (such as those in the *Behringer* range)
- good-quality headphones from BOSE, Sennheiser, Sony, Technics or other ranges
- all necessary cabling and connections.

The final mix will need to be recorded to a stereo mixer for submission on either CD or mini disc.

To begin with, you will need to think about the sounds to be recorded on the three (or more) tracks, and your own role within the performance; you can, of course, record anything from the minimum of one track through to all of them. You will also need to decide on the type of music to perform.

Objectives

You will learn:

what is involved in a technology-based performance

what resources you will need

how to acquire the necessary skills.

Key terms

Condenser microphone: these produce a high-quality recording for audio. They need a power source such as a battery, and often contain two microphones or diaphragms to enable recordings in a variety of patterns.

Dynamic microphone: these are relatively inexpensive, but tend to focus on a particular part of the frequency range.

Activity

As you make your decisions as to the final make-up of the three or more tracks to be recorded:

- make short recordings to improve your skills with the sequencer and/ or multi-track recorder

- produce different versions from the same inputted data, as you experiment with balance, effects and panning

- decide whether to concentrate on refining your skills in one area at a time

- gradually increase the length of the pieces you record as your skills improve

- play the results to other students, to your teacher, and to technicians, and listen to their feedback

- always keep copies of your work, with notes for reference.

You can choose from a wide range of musical genres. Your choice will depend on:

- your own tastes
- the performers available to you
- the software and hardware available.

Make sure that the hardware/software you use allows you to manipulate the inputted data in the ways required by the examination.

Depending on the style of the music, you might wish to use a drum machine (e.g. the Roland HD-1 V-Drums Lite or the Yamaha DD65 digital drum kit) to lay down a backing rhythm, or simply rely on a click track to ensure synchronisation of the tracks during performance.

Having decided on the music for your final submission, make sure that your chosen performers (if you are using others, as well as yourself) have plenty of time to learn it. If they are fellow students, they might prefer to complete this earlier in the year, before pressure builds up. Allow sufficient time to set up the recording. Have sample sessions before the final recording is made. Several takes may be necessary – in fact, it is better to do this if you are relying on others: you can decide later which version to manipulate for your coursework.

12.5 What are they looking for?

Technology-based performances have their own set of assessment criteria. You will be assessed on the quality of your performance in these areas:

- accuracy of pitch and rhythm, including evidence of close attention to performing and expressive detail
- care taken to ensure a good balance
- the use of an appropriate dynamic range
- the use of panning to obtain a clear recording and, where necessary, to separate sounds that use similar frequency ranges
- an awareness of the style required, including the use of effects such as reverb and delay where appropriate.

Each of these areas is marked out of six to give a total out of 30. Always aim to meet the descriptors for a mark in the top band (5–6 marks): set your sights on achieving the best result in all areas.

Objectives

You will learn:

about the assessment criteria for technology-based performances

how to get the marks in the highest bands

how to prepare the final recording.

Pitch and rhythm

The top band for this expects:

> 66 *Excellent accuracy of pitch and rhythm with close attention to all performing and expressive details, resulting in a musically satisfying performance.* 99

You are responsible for obtaining the various tracks that combine to make up your performance. Make sure they are performed accurately. Many recording machines enable you to adjust the recorded pitch so that it will come in line with that of other instruments and any MIDI channels you have used. Also, there is a 'transpose' function within most sequencing packages. You may need to use the quantising facility to ensure rhythmic accuracy.

Balance

To get the top band of marks here you will have to show:

> 66 *An excellent sense of balance throughout the recording.* 99

Your recording needs to be well balanced with no track either overpowering the others or being obscured. As the frequency of instances of poor balance or miscalculations increases, so your mark will move down through the bands.

Dynamic range

The top band requires:

> 66 *Excellent management of dynamics in ways completely appropriate to the music.* 99

It is expected that your music will cover a range of dynamics as appropriate to its style: you are assessed on how well you manage this range. With some instruments, you may need to use **compression**.

Panning

For the top marks here you will need to show:

> 66 *Judicious use of panning to gain a clear and effective recording.* 99

By using panning, you will be able to recreate the experience of a live performance with special separation of the tracks. It will produce a more 'spacious' sound as you 'place' each track either to one side or centrally for the listener. This will be essential if you are using sounds that are similar to each other: as in a flute trio, for example.

Awareness of style, including effects

Here, the top marks need you to show:

> 66 *Complete awareness of the stylistic requirements of the music with appropriate use of effects throughout the performance.* 99

The style of your chosen music will dictate to a large extent what you are able to do here. But, of course, you will need to apply some effects before the examiner can mark you on their use! Voice parts usually benefit from the application of some reverb, while you might also have to compensate for the acoustics in the room used for the recording.

Key terms
Compression: in audio recording, this is where the dynamic range of the performers is controlled to avoid distortion where the dynamic level is too high, and inaudibility where dynamics are too low.

AQA Examiner's tip
You need to practise during the course, keeping careful records of successful procedures so that you can repeat them in your final recording. Listen to your recording and gradually work towards achieving the best possible outcome in terms of the criteria described on these pages.

Activity
Just before you start work on your final performance: ■ play one of your finished practice performances to members of your group, to your teacher or to an ICT and/or audio technician   ■ make sure they have a copy of the assessment criteria   ■ ask them to mark your work   ■ discuss their marks, and come to conclusions on any areas which need further attention.

12

In this chapter you have learnt:

✔ an explanation of the skills required for Unit 3 (Performing Music)

✔ suggestions for ways of acquiring and improving skills

✔ strategies for improving performances

✔ the assessment criteria for acoustic and technology-based performances

✔ methods of accessing marks in the highest bands

✔ how to prepare for the final performances

✔ what is involved in a technology-based performance

✔ the implications in terms of resources.

Revision quiz

1. What is the minimum number of live performers needed for a group performance?

2. How long should each performance last?

3. What are the four areas of assessment for a solo acoustic performance?

4. How does the assessment for the group performance differ from that for the solo performance?

5. What are the five areas of assessment for a technology-based option?

6. What is meant by compression?

7. Name two types of sequencing software.

8. Name two notation/scoring packages.

9. What are the differences between a condenser microphone and a dynamic microphone?

10. Explain the difference(s) between a drum kit and a drum machine.

Preparing your performance

Objectives

In this chapter you will learn:

how to improve and master the techniques needed for your chosen pieces

how to work with others to rehearse for your final performances

methods of gaining and improving skills.

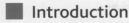

Introduction

Now you have decided on the pieces to be played, this chapter will focus on how to improve your performances, for both the acoustic and the technology-based options.

The focus of this chapter will be on practical activities to enable you to acquire and then improve the various techniques needed for the successful performance of your pieces. As most of you will have been playing or singing for some time, you might already have found a favourite style of music or an area where you think you perform best. This will have led to the acquisition of certain skills and techniques: this chapter will consider extending and fine-tuning these.

You will also learn ways of presenting your scores when traditionally notated music is either unavailable or inappropriate.

If you have performed already, you will have experienced a number of different styles and genres. Even if you are approaching GCSE Music without having received individual instrumental or vocal tuition, you will have taken part in practical musical activities during Key Stage 3 and will have become aware of some basic techniques. These may have covered how to stand and breathe while singing, how to play a recorder or tuned percussion instrument, how to use your fingers properly at a keyboard, or perhaps how to play a melody in time with a pre-set accompaniment and auto-rhythm.

Music from different periods and styles requires different approaches to performance, and part of the assessment reflects how well you show an understanding of the characteristics and style of your chosen music. For example, if you are to play the piano, in baroque music you might consider using the sustaining pedal less than when playing music from later periods. You would also need to practise the ornamentation (**trills**, **turns**, **mordents** and so on) very carefully.

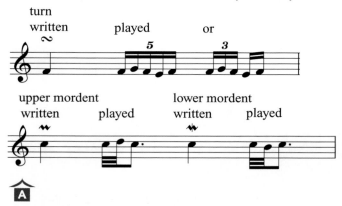

A

Music from later periods requires more use of graduated dynamics – **crescendo** and **diminuendo** – as well as gradual alterations of tempo through the application of **accelerando** and **rallentando/ritenuto/ ritardando**.

On orchestral strings, you might have to play **pizzicato** or use **double-stopping**. On string and brass instruments you might have to use a **mute** or, on strings or trombone, play a **glissando**.

Your choice needs to be based on your own technical ability and experience, after you have discussed things carefully with your teacher(s) and, for the group performance, others involved. Discuss, at the start of the GCSE course, your level of performing ability and consider how much you will be able to improve over four or five terms.

The top mark for Level of Demand is awarded for pieces above the equivalent of Grade 4 as set by the main boards such as the ABRSM, Trinity Guildhall and Rock School. Remember that there are only three marks available for this, so play music you will be confident with.

Having made your choices, learn your own part, seeking help to overcome any problems as soon as you become aware of them: don't leave this until the last moment. Find out who will be accompanying

Objectives

You will learn:

about techniques for practising and mastering technical skills

about techniques for rehearsing with others

about techniques for preparing for the final performance.

Key terms

Trill: the rapid alternation of two adjacent notes (see page 39)

Turn: the decoration of a written note by adding the pitches above and below. See example **A**.

Mordent: a single alternation with the note above (upper mordent) or below (lower mordent) the written note. See example **A**.

Crescendo: getting gradually louder.

Diminuendo: getting gradually quieter.

Accelerando: getting gradually faster.

Rallentando/ritenuto/ ritardando: getting gradually slower.

Pizzicato: plucking strings rather than playing them with a bow.

Double-stopping: playing on two strings at the same time.

Con sordino: playing with a mute – placing a piece of wood against the bridge of a string instrument, or altering the sound of a brass instrument by inserting a cone-shape into or covering the bell of the instrument.

Glissando: sliding from one note to the next – used on strings, trombone, harp and keyboard instruments,

you for your solo performance (unless you are playing a genuine solo on, for example, piano or classical guitar). Never miss out an intended accompaniment just because you find it difficult to play or sing along to.

Solo performances

If your solo performance is to be accompanied, arrange regular practice sessions with your accompanist so that you get to know what else is happening and exactly how your part fits in, particularly where there are rests to count. Make sure that you set the tempo at the beginning and that dynamics match. Practise changes of tempo and dynamics, and pay particular attention to any passages where it is tricky to fit your part against the accompaniment.

B Solo performance

Group performances

For your group performance, choose to work with a group you already know and/or have performed with. Other members of the group don't have to be GCSE students, or be assessed through the same piece of music. It is vital that everybody is happy with the choice of music and has plenty of time to learn his or her own part. Group rehearsals should be for making sure that all players are fitting together and understand how their part fits with what else is being played.

Check balance, phrasing, tuning, and keeping together (you can have a conductor if it makes things easier).

C Group performance

> **AQA Examiner's tip**
>
> Perform your pieces to different audiences to increase your own confidence and to gain feedback on how it went and how you might improve.

Points to remember

- Complete and sign the Candidate Record Form.
- Produce a final recording on CD or mini disc playable through a conventional machine.
- Submit a score of the music performed.
- Aim to give your best performance, but remember that, if it goes really wrong, you can play it again.
- Your teacher must assess your **live** performance.

For all performing options, you may use one of your own compositions as long as it is **not** submitted for assessment for either Unit 2 (Composing and Appraising) or Unit 4 (Composing).

13.2 Technology-based performances

Having decided to opt for using technology, you will need to master the various skills needed to gain the highest marks.

If you have decided to submit a technology-based performance, it will mean that you know you have access to the resources you will need (see page 164). Whether you use a sequencer or a multi-track recorder (or both), you must make sure that your performance contains a minimum of three tracks and that you have performed at least one of them in real or step time. You also need to decide whether all tracks will be entered via the sequencer, all via the multi-track recorder, or whether, for example, you will create a backing on the sequencer (e.g. piano and drum kit) and then record an audio track over it. In all cases, you must make clear on your Candidate Record Form (CRF) which hardware and software you use, as well as outlining the process of making your recording.

Using a sequencer

Most sequencers have a 'piano roll' facility that enables you to follow the input of each line and synchronise it with the others. These include Steinberg's Cubasis VST, Able MIDI Editor, Logic Pro 7 or Cakewalk Sonar 7. With these you can select your instrumental sounds, and enter **MIDI** data either by playing along in real time or by entering a note at a time in step time. Editing facilities are available to improve balance, dynamics and to synchronise the parts (*quantise*). You may want to start with a **click track**, to make it easier to keep tracks in time.

You should experiment with short performances until you have established the group of sounds you are happiest to use. These can be saved as a default arrangement: for example, in Cubasis VST, you set up your choice of MIDI/**VSTi**/audio tracks and then go to File>Save As and look in the folder for a song file called 'def'. You should then practise inputting short tracks and combinations of tracks before manipulating them to improve balance and panning, adding effects, ensuring the accuracy of each track, and so on. Refer to the assessment criteria as explained on pages 166–167.

Objectives

You will learn:

how your technology-based performance will be assessed

how to use a sequencer and/or a multi-track recorder

how to achieve the highest marks possible.

Key terms

MIDI: Musical Instrument Digital Interface – the means by which messages about what is played, in terms of data regarding pitch, duration, intensity, tempo and so on, are transmitted.

Click track: sometimes referred to as a metronome track, this provides a regular beat against which to play the other parts in real time.

VSTi: Virtual Studio instrument – a specific piece of software producing electronic sounds which create particular sets of sounds; some are based on synthesised technology while others rely on sampling.

Activity

1. Work with your chosen sequencing package to ensure that you fully understand everything it can do.

   Break down the process into several different steps, including:
   - inputting a track using step time and then using real time
   - inputting a track *with* a click track and *without*, to decide which makes the timing more accurate – or is the timing to be flexible?
   - inputting two tracks and then synchronising them, balancing them, adding effects, and so on.

Using a multi-track recorder

The use of a multi-track recorder opens up the possibilities of doing a multi-tracked audio performance of yourself, or of yourself with others, or exporting a sequenced backing part before adding an audio track. Your own performance on at least one track is essential and must form the central part of your planning.

A *Multi-track recorder*

Activity

2

- Set up your multi-track recorder and the necessary microphones and/or leads.
- Input one track, checking its dynamic range and ensuring there is neither distortion nor inaudible passages.
- Add a second track in the same way.
- Check and adjust balance and panning where necessary.
- Consider what effects might be applied, and experiment.
- If you are using pop instruments, consider the use of compression.
- Check the balance of frequencies across your recording and, if necessary, use **EQ** (**equalisation**).
- Decide the order in which you will record the tracks and do trial recordings.

Remember

- Complete and sign the Candidate Record Form.
- Produce a final recording on CD or mini disc playable through a conventional machine.
- Submit a score of the music performed.
- Make sure that your teacher can testify that the work is yours alone.

Key terms

EQ/equalisation: a function on multi-track recorders which allows you to adjust the relative balance of the frequencies present in your recording. Even the most basic multi-track recorder will have a mixing desk with three sections – low (bass), mid and high (treble). With these you can reduce or boost frequencies above or below a particular point (typically, bass below 100Hz, treble above 10 Hz, with mid EQ controlling the ranges in between these outer limits).

By now you should be ready to make your final performance, confident in your ability to achieve the required standard through your use of technology. Take care as you enter each track, re-recording as necessary so that you have the best possible basis from which to make your adjustments. Look at the assessment criteria again and decide what needs to be done with your recording to help you gain high marks: don't rush this part – plan ahead and allow yourself plenty of time for the editing/manipulation.

Although you should aim to submit a score using traditional staff notation wherever possible, there will be some instances where this is either unavailable or inappropriate.

The purpose of the score is to inform your teacher (who marks your performances initially) and then the moderator (who checks that mark against the standards set by the examination board) exactly what your role is and how it fits in with other performers or other elements in your technology-based performance. Where a traditionally notated score is not being used, you will need to provide detailed information by other means. See pages 114–21 in Chapter 7 and remind yourself of the advantages and disadvantages of the alternative methods: graphic notation, tab, a written account (annotation), or a combination of some or all of these (including staff notation for excerpts).

You will need to include, as appropriate:

- an outline of the form or structure
- details of the keys used
- details of chord progressions
- examples of different figurations, chord patterns or rhythms
- lyrics where appropriate, preferably with chord changes shown against them
- indications of tempo, use of dynamics, any particular features of articulation
- instrumentation
- full details of your own part, so that its level of difficulty can be assessed for an acoustic performance and your role in all performances can be appreciated.

Make sure that your part in the recorded performance is clear, without artificially manipulating the balance to isolate your playing, as this will have a negative influence on marks.

What follows are suggested outlines or starting points for annotations. If the annotation is to accompany your technology-based performance, you should also include details of the equipment used and the process of recording, including:

- the order in which tracks were laid down
- the equipment used (hardware and software)
- use of panning, EQ, and so on, perhaps in the form of a table.

Annotation of performance

Learning the music from a recording

It is possible that you learned the music from listening to its performance by the original artist(s) rather than from notation. In this case, the original version should be submitted as a benchmark recording, but you must make clear your role in the performance to be assessed, and to what extent you aimed to reproduce the style of that original version. If your performance is to a backing CD, a sort of

Objectives

You will learn:

about ways of presenting your scores when traditionally notated music is either unavailable or inappropriate.

karaoke-style performance, you should again try to submit the version with its original performer(s).

Give information as to your intentions in terms of phrasing and dynamics, articulation and performing techniques. If you are accompanied by live musicians, give details if their performance differs from the original. If at all possible, still submit the sheet music, but indicate that it is supplied merely as a guide to the performance and that yours will differ in the ways you specify.

Learning the music from tab, by imitation or other methods

Even if tab or other forms of notation are included as part of your submission, you will need to give additional detail to explain to your teacher and the moderator exactly what your role was and what your intentions were (refer to page 118 on the use of tab scores). Here are some examples of possible openings of performance commentaries.

Annotations to accompany performances

Example 1: opening of commentary

A performance of 'Hero', originally recorded by Mariah Carey

Submitting a copy of the sheet music and a benchmark recording by Mariah Carey

My performance is accompanied just by piano. I have tried to put real feeling into my performance and don't always stick to the notes in the sheet music but I don't try to copy all of the vocal improvisations done by Mariah Carey. I have tried to make this my own interpretation by altering the tune a bit every time the chorus comes back. I think that this is a really passionate song and have tried to show this in my singing. I have used dynamics to contrast the more thoughtful sections with the chorus in particular.

Example 2: opening of commentary

A performance of 'Stairway to Heaven', based on the recording by Led Zeppelin

Submitting a tab version downloaded from www.Ultimate-Guitar.com

This is performed just by me, playing acoustic guitar and singing. I see this as a quiet, thoughtful, reflective song and have tried to show this. I am using a semi-acoustic guitar. The recording is made with two microphones, one for the guitar, one for my voice. It was recorded onto two channels of a multi-track recorder after some trial recordings were made to check the balance of the two parts. Afterwards, slight reverb was added to both

parts to give a slightly richer sound. The dynamics don't change much because I think this is more in keeping with the way I wanted to perform this song.

Example 3: opening of commentary

A performance of an instrumental written by me and the rest of my group. The line-up is lead guitar (played by me), rhythm guitar, bass and drums. The opening is a riff (in tab and notation) which I play loudly:

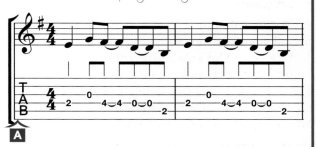

This is repeated four times and then the drums enter with a steady rock beat. At the same time, the rhythm guitar adds chords of Em and Bm7 while the bass plays:

The rest of the piece is in the form: verse, pre-chorus, chorus, verse, second pre-chorus, chorus, lead guitar improvisation using A minor pentatonic, pre-chorus, chorus with the last line repeated as the music fades out.

13

In this chapter you have learnt:

✔ about practising and mastering technical skills

✔ about rehearsing with others

✔ how to prepare for the final performance

✔ how your technology-based performance will be assessed

✔ how to use a sequencer and/or a multi-track recorder

✔ how to achieve the highest marks possible

✔ ways of presenting your scores when traditionally notated music is either unavailable or inappropriate.

Revision quiz

1. Explain the main difference in the way a *trill* was performed in the baroque period compared with later periods.

2. Explain the difference between an *upper mordent* and a *lower mordent*.

3. Which family of instruments can play *pizzicato* and use *double-stopping*?

4. For acoustic performances, what standard of music will gain the top mark for Level of Demand?

5. Give as many reasons as you can why it is important to arrange several rehearsals with your accompanist (solo performance) and other members of the group (group performance).

6. Name two sequencing packages.

7. What is meant by the term MIDI?

8. What is a VSTi?

9. What is EQ and why is it used?

10. Why is staff notation the preferred choice for a musical score?

11. Why is it important to give as much detail as possible about your part in the performance on your Candidate Record Form?

12. On page 174, eight bullet points were given about the range of information needed in an annotation: how many can you remember? (When you have done as many as possible, refer back to the page).

13. What additional information is needed for a technology-based performance? (If you cannot remember the three areas listed, refer to page 174.)

14. Can you play one of your own compositions as a performance piece for the examination?

15. Can you submit the same piece as your composition?

kerboodle!

CD track listing

Spread/ Book ref (CD/Track)	Title and copyright
2.1 01 (1/1)	'Olin lacus colueram' Carl Orff, Carmina Burana 'Olim lacus colueram', Thomas Randle, Tenor, Bournemouth Symphony Orchestra, Conductor: Marin Alsop, Bournemouth Symphony Chorus, Bournemouth Symphony Youth Chorus, Highcliffe Junior Choir; Track (p) 1988 – 2009 licensed courtesy of Naxos Rights International Ltd
3.2 2 (1/2)	Excerpts from Music for the Royal Fireworks George Frideric Handel, Music for the Royal Fireworks, Menuet I & II, Orchestra, Capella Istropolitana, conductor Bohdan Warchal; Track (p) 1988 – 2009 licensed courtesy of Naxos Rights International Ltd
3.2 3 (1/3)	Brandenburg Concerto no. 2 in F major, 2nd movement ohann Sebastian Bach, Brandenburg Concerto No. 2 in F major, I. Allegro ,Cologne Chamber Orchestra, conductor Helmut Muller-Bruhl; Track (p) 1988 – 2009 licensed courtesy of Naxos Rights International Ltd
3.2 4 (1/4)	Canon in G Johann Pachelbel, Canon and Gigue, Cologne Chamber Orchestra, conductor Helmut Muller-Bruhl; Track (p) 1988 – 2009 licensed courtesy of Naxos Rights International Ltd
3.2 5 (1/5)	'Spring' from The Four Seasons, 1st movement Antonio Vivaldi, The 4 Seasons: Violin Concerto in E major, 'La primavera' (Spring), I. Allegro, Capella Istropolitana Orchestra, conductor Stephen Gunzenhauser, Takako Nishizaki violin; Track (p) 1988 – 2009 licensed courtesy of Naxos Rights International Ltd. Track (p) 1988 – 2009 licensed courtesy of Naxos Rights International Ltd
3.3 6 (1/6)	Clarinet Concerto, 2nd movement Wolfgang Amadeus Mozart, Clarinet Concerto in A major, II. Adagio, Vienna Mozart Academy, conductor Wildner, Johannes, Ernst Ottensamer clarinet; Track (p) 1988 – 2009 licensed courtesy of Naxos Rights International Ltd
3.3 7 (1/7)	Horn Concerto no. 4 in E-flat major, 3rd movement Wolfgang Amadeus Mozart, Horn Concerto No. 4 in E flat major, III. Rondo: Allegro vivace, Philharmonia Orchestra, conductor Herbert von Karajan, Dennis Brain horn; Track (p) 1988 – 2009 licensed courtesy of Naxos Rights International Ltd
3.3 8 (1/8)	Piano Concerto no. 1 in B-flat minor, 1st movement Pyotr Il'yich Tchaikovsky, Piano Concerto No. 1 in B flat minor, I. Allegro non troppo e molto maestoso – Allegro con spirito. Slovak Radio Symphony Orchestra, conductor Ondrei Lenard, Joseph Banowetz Piano; Track (p) 1988 – 2009 licensed courtesy of Naxos Rights International Ltd
3.4 9 (1/9)	Credo, from 'Nelson' Mass Josef Haydn, Mass No. 11 in D minor, Nelson Mass, Credo: Credo in unum Deum, Hungarian Radio Chorus, conductor, Nicholas Esterhazy Sinfonia, conductor Bels Drahos; Track (p) 1988 – 2009 licensed courtesy of Naxos Rights International Ltd
3.4 10 (1/10)	Excerpt from Rex tremendae Wolfgang Amadeus Mozart, Requiem, 'Rex tremendae', Leipzig Chamber Orchestra, conductor Morten Schuldt-Jensen, Gewandhaus Chamber Choir; Track (p) 1988 – 2009 licensed courtesy of Naxos Rights International Ltd
3.4 11 (1/11)	Excerpt from O sacrum convivium Thomas Tallis, Mass for four voices, Motet 'O sacrum convivium', Oxford Camerata, conductor Jeremy Summerly; Track (p) 1988 – 2009 licensed courtesy of Naxos Rights International Ltd
3.4 12 (1/12)	Excerpt from 'Behold a virgin shall conceive', from Messiah George Frideric Handel, Messiah, 'Behold a Virgin Shall Conceive ... O Thou that Tellest Good Tidings to Zion', Scholars Baroque Ensemble; Track (p) 1988 – 2009 licensed courtesy of Naxos Rights International Ltd
3.4 13 (1/13)	'Now is the month of maying' Thomas Morley, 'Now is the month of Maying' Conductor: John Rutter, Cambridge Singers
3.5 14 (1/14)	Excerpt from 'One fine day', from Madame Butterfly Giacomo Puccini, Madama Butterfly, Act II – Un bel di, vedremo, libretto: Luigi Illica and Guiseppe Giacosa, Slovak Radio Symphony Orchestra, conductor Alexander Rahbari, Miriam Gaucci soprano; Track (p) 1988 – 2009 licensed courtesy of Naxos Rights International Ltd
3.5 15 (1/15)	Excerpt from 'Au fond du temple saint', from The Pearl Fishers Georges Bizet, Les pecheurs de perles, Act I: Au fond du temple saint, Slovak Radio Symphony Orchestra, conductor, Johannes Wildner, Janez Lotric tenor, Igor Morozov baritone; Track (p) 1988 – 2009 licensed courtesy of Naxos Rights International Ltd
3.5 16 (1/16)	Excerpt from 'Nähe des Geliebten' 'Nähe des Geliebten', Franz Schubert, licensed courtesy Hyperion Records, 1984, GBJY 8413204
3.5 17 (1/17)	'From far, from eve and morning' Ralph Vaughan-Williams, On Wenlock Edge, Duke Quartet, Anthony Rolfe-Johnson tenor, Graham Johnson piano; Track (p) 1988 – 2009 licensed courtesy of Naxos Rights International Ltd.
3.5 18 (1/18)	'O ruddier than the cherry', from Acis and Galatea George Frideric Handel, Acis and Galatea, 'O Ruddier than the Cherry', Scholars Baroque Ensemble, conductor David van Asch, David van Asch bass-baritone; Track (p) 1988 – 2009 licensed courtesy of Naxos Rights International Ltd
3.6 19 (1/19)	Excerpt from String Quartet op. 95 in F minor, 1st movement Ludwig van Beethoven, String Quartet No. 11 in F minor, 'Serioso', I. Allegro con brio, Kodaly Quartet; Track (p) 1988 – 2009 licensed courtesy of Naxos Rights International Ltd
3.6 20 (1/20)	Excerpt from String Quartet no. 4, 4th movement Bela Bartok, String Quartet No. 4, Allegretto pizzicato, Vermeer Quartet; Track (p) 1988 – 2009 licensed courtesy of Naxos Rights International Ltd
3.6 21 (1/21)	'Trout' Quintet, theme with variations Franz Schubert, 'Trout' Quintet, Jeno Jando, piano, Kodaly Quartet, Ystvan Toth, double bass
3.7 22 (1/22)	Piano Sonata in C-sharp minor op. 27, no. 2, 'Moonlight' Ludwig van Beethoven, Piano sonata opus 27 No. 2 in C-Sharp minor, Jeno Jando piano; Track (p) 1988 – 2009 licensed courtesy of Naxos Rights International Ltd

3.7 23 (1/23) Excerpt from Violin Sonata no. 5 in F major, op. 24, 'Spring'

Ludwig van Beethoven, Violin Sonata No. 5 in F major, 'Spring' I. Allegro, Tkako Nishizaki violin, Jeno Jando piano; Track (p) 1988 – 2009 licensed courtesy of Naxos Rights International Ltd

4.1 24 (1/24) 'Careless Love Blues'

Bessie Smith, remastered by Peter Nickol

4.8 25 (1/25) Jaws

Jaws - "Original Motion Picture Score", Composer: John Williams, Performed by Joel McNeely and The Royal Scottish National Orchestra, (VSD-6078), Courtesy of Varèse Sarabande Records, Inc.

5.1 26 (1/26) Osvaldo Chacón excerpt from 'Vacunala'

Taken from Salsa Timbre Cubana' Osvaldo chacon Vacunala, P & C 2008 Licensed courtesy of ARC Music Productions Ltd

5.2 27 (1/27) Excerpt from 'Uma Ilanga Liyo'

Uma Ilanga Liyo Shone (Soweto Gospel Choir) P&C 2006. Licensed courtesy of ARC Music Productions Ltd

5.3 28 (1/28) 'Ubumwe'

UBUMWE (DR), Les tambours du Burundi © Boneka Productions (p) Sunset-France www.playasound.com

5.5 29 (1/29) 'Master of the Indian Bansuri' Pandit Ronu Majumdar

Taken from Raga Bhim Palasi P&C 2007. Licensed courtesy of ARC Music Productions Ltd

5.5 30 (1/30) 'Bhangra fever'

MIDIval Punditz – Bhangra Fever , Composed by Gaurav Raina and Tapan Raj, Published by Six Degrees Beats Publishing (BMI), Courtesy of Six Degrees Records (www.sixdegreesrecords.com)

7.1 31 (2/1) Shifting rhythms

© Andrew S Coxon

7.3 32 (2/2) Voiles, no. 2

Claude Debussy, Preludes, Book 1 Voiles No. 2, Yukie Nagai Piano; Track (p) 1988 – 2009 licensed courtesy of Naxos Rights International Ltd

7.14 33 (2/3) Trumpet Concerto in E-flat major, last movement

Josef Haydn, Trumpet Concerto in E flat major, III. Finale: Allegro, Cologne Chamber Orchestra, conductor Helmut Muller-Bruhl, Jurgen Schuster trumpet; Track (p) 1988 – 2009 licensed courtesy of Naxos Rights International Ltd

7.14 34 (2/4) Violin Concerto in D major op. 61, 1st movement

Ludwig van Beethoven, Violin Concerto in D major, III. Rondo: Allegro, Berlin State Opera Orchestra, conductor Leo Blech, Fritz Kreisler violin; Track (p) 1988 – 2009 licensed courtesy of Naxos Rights International Ltd

7.14 35 (2/5) Piano Concerto no. 2 in C minor op. 18, 1st

Sergie Rachmaninov, Piano Concerto No. 2 in C minor op. 18 Polish National Radio Symphony Orchestra, conductor Antoni Wit, Bernd Glemser piano; Track (p) 1988 – 2009 licensed courtesy of Naxos Rights International Ltd

7.14 36 (2/6) 'The watchman's song'

Edvard Grieg, Lyric Pieces, Book 1, Op. 12; Einar Steen-Nokleberg piano; Track (p) 1988 – 2009 licensed courtesy of Naxos Rights International Ltd

7.14 37 (2/7) 'The Trumpet Shall Sound', from Messiah

George Frideric Handel, Messiah, 'The Trumpet Shall Sound', Scholars Baroque Ensemble; Track (p) 1988 – 2009 licensed courtesy of Naxos Rights International Ltd

7.14 38 (2/8) Horn Concerto no. 4 in E-flat, last movement

Wolfgang Amadeus Mozart, Horn Concerto No. 4 in E flat major, III. Rondo: Allegro vivace, Philharmonia Orchestra, conductor Herbert von Karajan, Dennis Brain horn; Track (p) 1988 – 2009 licensed courtesy of Naxos Rights International Ltd

7.15 39 (2/9) The pop-style group

© Andrew S Coxon

7.15 40 (2/10) The wind ensemble

© Andrew S Coxon

Openings of exemplar music for each Area of Study
© Andrew S Coxon

8.2 41 (2/11) AoS1: rhythm & metre

8.2 42 (2/12) AoS2: harmony & tonality

8.2 43 (2/13) AoS3: texture & melody

8.2 44 (2/14) AoS4: timbre & dynamics

8.2 45 (2/15) AoS5: structure & form

Continuations of exemplar music for each Area of Study
© Andrew S Coxon

8.3 46 (2/16) AoS1: rhythm & metre

8.3 47 (2/17) AoS2: harmony & tonality

8.3 48 (2/18) AoS3: texture & melody

8.3 49 (2/19) AoS4: timbre & dynamics

8.3 50 (2/20) AoS5: structure & form

The following are tracks you will need to source yourself:

4.3 'Blowin' in the wind' by Bob Dylan

4.4 'She loves you' by the Beatles

4.4 'Strawberry Fields forever' by the Beatles

4.4 'I can't get no satisfaction' by the Rolling Stones

4.5 Albums by Pink Floyd or concept albums such as The Six Wives of Henry VIII by Rick Wakeman, or Pictures at an exhibition by Emerson, Lake and Palmer

4.5 'Child in Time' by Deep Purple

4.5 Dark Side of the Moon by Pink Floyd

4.6 'Good Life' by Kanye West

4.6 'Bring him home' from the musical Les Misérables

5.1 Examples of calypso music, for example by Lord Kitchener and Mighty Sparrow

5.1 Examples of live steel band music

5.2 'One love' by Bob Marley

5.2 Songs from Africa

7.1 African and Caribbean Music, music by John Adams and Steve Reich, 'Take five' or 'Unsquare dance' by Dave Brubeck

7.4 music of Star Wars, Atonement or Gladiator, Haydn's Trumpet Concerto in E flat and its slow movement, 'She loves you' by the Beatles and 'Stairway to Heaven' by Led Zeppelin

7.5 Songs by the Beatles, including 'Love me do', 'She loves you' and 'A day in the life'.

7.5 Canon by Pachelbel, or 'I'll CU when U get there' by Coolio

7.7 Canon and Gigue by Pachelbel

7.7 Spring, Summer, Autumn or Winter from The Four Seasons by Vivaldi

7.7 The slow movement from the Trumpet Concerto in E flat by Haydn

7.7 'The Erl King' by Schubert

7.7 'Nessun dorma' from Turandot by Pucini

7.7 'She loves you' by the Beatles

7.7 'Bohemian rhapsody' by Queen

7.7 'Tainted love' by Soft Cell

7.7 'Stairway to Heaven' by Led Zeppelin

7.7 Excerpts from the sound track to Star Wars by John Williams and/or Lord of the Rings by Howard Shore

7.7 Excerpts from The Rough Guide to the Music of India

■ Suggested listening

As well as the tracks on the CD, here is a list of other pieces you could listen to, organised by the three Strands of Learning. These are not set works and you will not be tested specifically on them. They are just a starting point. Ask your teacher to suggest other pieces to listen to, and try to hear as much music as possible from other sources (see the suggested list of radio stations on page 127, for example).

The Western Classical tradition

Baroque orchestral music

Bach	Brandenburg Concerto No. 2 in F, BWV 1047
Handel	*Water Music*

The concerto

Tchaikovsky	Violin Concerto No. 1 in D Op. 35
Shostakovitch	Piano Concerto No. 2 in F Op. 102

Music for voices

Gibbons	'The Silver Swan'
Puccini	'Nessun Dorma' from *Turandot*

Chamber music

Haydn	String Quartet in C Op. 76 No. 3 *'Emperor'*
Schubert	Piano Quintet Op. 114, D 667, *'The Trout'*
Stravinsky	8 Miniatures for 15 Players

The sonata

Scarlatti	Piano Sonata in G minor *'Cat's Fugue'*
Chopin	Piano Sonata No. 2 in B flat minor Op. 35

Popular music of the 20th and 21st centuries

Blues

Johnson	'Come on in my kitchen'	Robert Johnson
King/Josea	'You upset me baby'	BB King
Clapton	'Sunshine of your love'	Cream

Popular music of the 1960s

Lennon/McCartney	'She loves you'	Beatles
Jagger/Richards	'I can't get no satisfaction'	Rolling Stones
Waters	'Money'	Pink Floyd

Rock music, R'n'B, hip-hop

Page/Plant	'Stairway to Heaven'	Led Zeppelin
West	'Gold digger'	Kanye West
Ne-Yo	'Take a bow'	Rihanna

Music theatre

Schwartz	'Defying gravity'	from *Wicked*
Bart	'I'm reviewing the situation'	from *Oliver*
Lloyd-Webber	'Any dream will do'	from *Joseph and the Amazing Technicolor Dreamcoat*

Film music

Williams	*Star Wars*
Marianelli	*Atonement*
Zimmer	*Gladiator*

World Music

Music of the Caribbean

World of Music: Caribbean	various artists
The Rough Guide to World Music, Vol 2	various artists

Music of Africa

The *Very Best of Africa*	various artists
The Rough Guide to the Music of South Africa	various artists
The Spirit of Africa	various artists

Music of India

The Very Best of India	various artists
The Rough Guide to the Music of India	various artists
The Sounds of India	Ravi Shankar

Quiz answers

① The new GCSE course

Revision quiz, page 12

1) 1 Listening to and appraising music, 2 Composing and appraising music, 3 Performing music and 4 Composing music. 2) AO1 Performing skills, AO2 Composing skills and AO3 Listening and appraising skills. 3) AO1 performing/realising with technical control, expression and interpretation, AO2 creating and developing musical ideas with technical control and coherence, AO3 analysing and evaluating music using musical terminology. 4) Performing music is worth 40%. 5) Composing and appraising. 6) No: each is worth 10% to make 20% for the whole unit. 7) Acoustic and technology-based. 8) Any written format that is appropriate to the music presented. See page 114 for further details. 9) Five. 10) Three. 11) Unit 2. 12) 3 Performing music and 4 Composing music.

② The five Areas of Study and three Strands of Learning

Revision quiz, page 44

1) A rhythm is how different lengths of sound are combined to produce patterns; a metre is a regular pattern of beats. See page 14. 2) Two or more rhythms played at the same time. See page 17. 3) Unwritten tempo changes. See page 17. 4) A note sustained while the harmony changes. See page 19. 5) Dominant (V) and tonic (I). 6) Modulation. 7) Chordal; melody with accompaniment. See page 24. 8) Interweaving melody lines. See page 24. 9) Special notes used in blues music, created by mixing notes of the major and minor scales. See page 28. 10) Short repeated rhythmic or melodic phrase. See page 29. 11) Phrase repeated at a different pitch, often by step. See page 28. 12) Conjunct. 13) Ornament leaning on to the melody note. See page 27. 14) Plucking a string instrument. 15) Crescendo or cresc.

③ The Western Classical tradition

3.2 Listening quiz, page 49

1) Polyphonic/contrapuntal. 2) 2/4 or 4/4. 3) Trumpet.

3.4 Listening quiz, page 53

1) Harmonic/homophonic, a cappella. 2) Dominant.
3) 4/4, 2/4, 2/2.

3.5 Listening quiz, page 55

1) Minor. 2) 2/4, 4/4, 2/2. 3) Octaves 4) Perfect (V–I).

3.6 Listening quiz, page 57

1) Violin, viola, cello, double bass, piano. 2) Violin. 3) Fourth.
4) Major. 5) Harmonic/homophonic.

3.7 Listening quiz, page 59

1) Mostly conjunct. 2) Broken chords. 3) Diatonic.

Revision quiz, page 60

1) 1600–1750. 2) Harpsichord. 3) Accompanying instrument that plays a part based on the bass line of the music. See page 49. 4) Strings/violins. 5) Suite. 6) Minuet. See page 48. 7) Concertino; ripieno. 8) Dynamics, timbre, texture, between solo/tutti, or concertino/ripieno. 9) Quintet. 10) 'Sounded' or 'played'.

④ Popular music of the 20th and 21st centuries

4.1 Listening activity, page 63

1a) Some pauses in the vocal line; other small changes to the vocal/instrumental parts. They add variation to the repeats, so that the music becomes less predictable. These are only slight changes, creating an effective balance between contrast and repetition. They keep the listener engaged.
1b) Trumpet, trombone.

4.4 Listening quiz, page 69

1) Distortion. 2) Makes it sound raw, more aggressive.
3) Riff or scalic. 4) Syncopated 5) b.

4.5 Listening quiz, page 71

1a) Ostinato. 1b) Synthesiser. 1c) Make it sound psychedelic, unusual, experimental.

4.6 Listening quiz, page 72

1a) Riff. 1b) Major.

4.7 Listening quiz, page 73

2a) Makes it sound strained, tense. 2b) Sounds like crying, pleading, emotional. 2c) ABA. 2d) Major. 2e) Octave.

4.8 Listening activity, page 75

1) Dissonant/chromatic. 2) Conjunct. 3) Harp. 4) Pedal, syncopation. 5) From chimes, timpani; bass drum, woodblock, cymbals.

Revision quiz, page 76

1) Three. 2) Blue notes. 3) Bvox. 4) Strophic; verse/chorus. 5) AABA. 6) Rhythm played on beats 2 and 4. See page 70. 7) Guitar chords containing only the root and fifth. 8) Musical 'tag' given to a person, object etc. See page 74. 9) Sample of sound that is repeated continuously. See page 72. 10) Electronic device that creates sounds electronically. See page 70.

5 World music

5.1 Listening quiz, page 79

1) Dotted rhythms; syncopation. 2) Piano. 3) 8. 4) Female. 5) Chorus/verse.

5.5 Listening quiz, page 87

1) Traditional instruments (drums, shenhai); repeated rhythm; shouts of 'hoi' or 'hi'. 2) Electronic effects (e.g. reverb/delay); sequencer; electronic drum beats. 3) 4/4. 4) Ostinato. 5) 2 and 4.

Revision questions, page 88

1) Son; rumba. 2) Clave rhythm. 3) 2 and 4 (backbeat). 4) Electric guitar. 5) Reverse strumming. 6) A solo phrase answered by other singers/players. 7) A texture combining several contrasting rhythms. 8) Rhythms which use accents and syncopation to cut across each other and the beat. 9) Rag. 10) Alap; gat.

6 Introduction to composition

Revision quiz, page 94

1) Metre; harmony; texture; dynamics; structure. 2) The Western Classical tradition; Popular music of the 20th and 21st centuries; World music. 3) Unit 2: Composing and Appraising. 4) Two. 5) No. 6) See list on page 90. 7) Write about the process of composing as well as your finished piece. Refer to the recording process; problems you met along the way and how they were overcome; the success of your composition in terms of the AoS you chose and its link to the strand; how your composition relates to the context of that focus within the strand.

7 Developing composing skills

Revision quiz, page 128

1) Rhythm: the use of notes of different lengths; different combinations of note values. Metre: the number of beats in a bar. Harmony: the combination of pitched sounds. Tonality: the sense of having a tonal centre, a sense of key, of belonging to a key or mode. Texture: the number of sounds heard together. Melody: the organisation of different pitches and rhythms into a pattern. Timbre: the sound of the different instruments and voices. Dynamics: differences in volume. Structure: the overall shape of a composition. Form: accepted structures for composition. 2) Simple: crotchet beat divided into groups of two quavers. Compound: dotted crotchet beat divided into groups of three quavers. 3) Where notes that do not fall on the regular beats are accented. 4) Diatonic: written using major or minor keys; chromatic: uses notes in addition to those which would be found in a major or minor scale or a mode. 5. Perfect, plagal, imperfect, interrupted. See page 20. 6) The final chord of music in a minor key has a major third rather than minor. 7) Major: music based on a major scale (see page 23); minor: music based on a minor scale (see page 23); modal: music using an earlier form of scale (see page 23). 8) Sharps: FCGDAEB; flats: BEADGCF. 9) Harmonic/homophonic: different parts sing and/or play different notes but move in the same rhythm; contrapuntal/polyphonic: different parts sing and/or play different notes using different rhythms. See page 24. 10) Conjunct: movement of pitch by step; disjunct: movement of pitch by leaps/jumps. 11) Strings.

12) *pp p mp mf f ff*. 13) Binary: AB; ternary: ABA; rondo: ABACA; arch-form: ABCBA.
14) A bass pattern/melody that is repeated while parts above alter. 15) Strophic: keeps the same tune for each verse; through-composed: has new music throughout.

8 Choosing the area of composition

Revision quiz, page 136

1) Two. 2) Ten. 3) AQA. 4) No. 5) Any three from: binary, ternary, call and response, rondo, theme and variations, arch-form, sonata, minuet/scherzo and trio, strophic, through-composed, da capo aria, cyclic, popular song form, ground bass. 6) Major; minor; modal . 7) Primary: based on the first, fourth and fifth notes of the scale; secondary: based on the second, third and sixth notes of the scale. See page 130. 8) Major seventh: covers 11 semitones (e.g. C–B); minor seventh: covers 10 semitones (e.g. D–C); diminished seventh: covers 9 semitones (e.g. D♯–C or C♯ to B♭). 9) A rounding-off section. 10) Pitched percussion: timpani, piano, celeste/celesta, glockenspiel, metallophone, vibraphone, xylophone, marimba, tubular bells, steel drums, etc.; unpitched percussion: snare drum, tom toms, side drum, bass drum, cymbal(s), gong, castanets, maracas, whip, cabasa, guiro, wood block, etc. 11) Piano, harpsichord, organ, harp, guitar, string instruments (double-stopping), accordion, bandoneon, celeste/celesta, any tuned percussion, etc. 12) Where the parts are gradually added/increased; built up by recording tracks separately and then combining them. 13) A rhythmic piano accompaniment pattern. See page 24. 14) Two balancing phrases, one 'asking' and the other 'answering'. See page 100. 15) AoS2: rhythm and metre; AoS3: texture and melody; AoS4: timbre and dynamics; AoS5: structure and form. 16) A texture combining several contrasting rhythms. 17) It changes key. 18) It gives your music direction; it will usually need a balancing modulation to return to the original key. 19) A melody added to an existing/earlier melody. 20) To provide contrast with the main theme.

9 Appraising your composition

Revision quiz, page 144

1) False. 2) No: you should respond to all questions in your appraisal. 3) The board. 4) You will write about why you chose the particular focus within the strand. 5) Because you can prepare your appraisal in advance and take your notes into the exam. 6) Check back with the list on page 139. 7) Check back with the list on page 143. 8) Alter the name of the instrument (e.g. from 'Flute' to 'Flute sounds'). 9) Check back with the lists on page 133. 10) Up to two hours.

10 Managing your time

Revision quiz, page 150

1) False. 2) True. 3) False: you have up to two hours. 4) True, but you cannot bring your composition in to the supervised sessions or remove any work from them; for your appraisal, you can bring in all the notes you have prepared. 5) False. 6) False. 7) False. 8) False. 9) False. 10) True, but other forms of notation are also acceptable. 11) True. 12) True.

⑪ Making choices

Revision quiz, page 156

1) Your ability to perform/realise music with technical control, expression and interpretation. 2) Two. 3) Above Grade 4. 4) 10%. 5) None – each is worth 30%. 6) Three. 7) One. 8) The separation of sounds to create a clear recording. See page 155. 9) Real time: where the sequencer records the actual rhythms that you play; step time: where you input the notes one at a time. See page 153. 10) Where playing two instruments simultaneously affects the level of demand of your performance. See page 154.

⑫ Developing skills

Revision quiz, page 168

1) Two. 2) No longer than five minutes. 3) Level of demand; accuracy; communication; interpretation. 4) Communication and interpretation are grouped into one area for assessment; ensemble is introduced as a new area for assessment. 5) Check back with the list on page 166. 6) Control of the performers' dynamic range in recording. See page 167. 7) CubaseSX (Steinberg); Logic Pro 7; Cakewalk Sonar 7; keyboards with built-in sequencing capability. 8) Sibelius; Coda Finale 2005; Garageband. 9) Condenser: needs a power source and often contains two microphones or diaphragms; dynamic: tends to focus on a particular part of the frequency range. See page 164. 10) Drum kit: acoustic; drum machine: electronic/digital.

⑬ Preparing your performance

Revision quiz, page 176

1) Baroque: trill started on the note above; later: trill started on the written note. 2) The upper mordent moves up first and the lower mordent moves down. See page 170. 3) Strings. 4) Above the equivalent of Grade 4. 5) Check back with the information given on page 171. 6) CubaseSX (Steinberg); Logic Pro 7; Cakewalk Sonar 7. 7) Musical Instrument Digital Interface. See page 172. 8) Virtual studio instrument. See page 172. 9) Equalisation; used to adjust balance of frequencies. See page 173. 10) It can convey a lot of information/detail concisely. 11) So that your teacher and the moderator can assess your performance accurately. 12) Check back with page 174. 13) Check back with p174. 14) Yes, if it contains sufficient technical, expressive and interpretative demands. 15) No.

Glossary

A

accent: a type of articulation where a particular note is to be stressed:

acciaccatura: also referred to as crush notes: a note of decoration played in as short a time as possible, i.e. crushed in:

added seventh: adding a further note to a triad, a 7th above the root

Alberti bass: an accompaniment played in the left hand of a keyboard part, using broken chords to produce a regular rhythmic pattern

antiphonal: (literally sounding across) used to describe the effect produced by the use of different groups of performers separated spatially

appoggiatura: (i) a note of decoration which is written in smaller type but given its full notated value, this value being taken from the following note; (ii) an accented but not harmonised note which resolves by step up or down

arch shape, arch form: music in at least five sections, in the form A B C B A

arpeggio: playing the notes of a chord by spreading them out (usually from the bottom), a feature commonly used by piano, harp and guitar

articulation: the addition of specific instructions for performance, such as accents, staccato and tenuto

augmentation: (i) the doubling of note values; (ii) the widening of an interval

B

bar: a small unit of music; the number of beats in each bar is shown by the time signature

binary form: music in two sections, each of which is similar in style; the first section (A) may modulate (e.g. to the dominant); the second section (B) will return to the tonic. Section B might include a repeat of or reference to Section A. Each section is normally repeated

bi-rhythm: the use of two different rhythms together

blue note: a note that has been altered/flattened in blues music; most frequently it is the 3rd, 5th or 7th notes of the scale which are flattened

bpm: beats per minute

broken chord: normally referring to a type of accompaniment figure derived from spreading the notes of a chord, as in this example:

C

cadence: a progression of (usually) two chords which end a musical phrase (see also: perfect, plagal, imperfect, interrupted)

cadenza: a solo vocal or instrumental passage improvising on music previously heard in the movement. Nowadays, most cadenzas are worked out in advance, with many written by the original composer.

call and response: the opening phrase is answered or completed by one or more other musicians

canonic: imitation, where performers enter with the same tune before the previous entry has finished, producing an overlapping effect

chamber group: small group of players or singers, for example a string quartet

chamber music: music written for small groups of players or singers

chord: two or more notes sounded together

chord symbol: used to describe a chord in a simple manner; this example shows how they can be used to identify major, minor and dominant seventh chords:

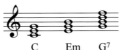

chromatic: music written using both the black and white notes of the piano; a scale which moves always by semitone; the alteration by a semitone of the notes of a diatonic scale

coda/codetta: a rounding-off section

compound time: time signatures based on a dotted crotchet beat, divided into three quavers, for example 6/8

compression: in audio recording, this is where the dynamic range of the performers is controlled to avoid both distortion where the dynamic level is too high and inaudibility where dynamics are too low

con arco (with a bow): using a bow to produce a note on a string instrument

con sordino (muted): placing a piece of wood against the bridge of a string instrument or altering the sound of a brass instrument by inserting a cone-shape into or covering the bell of the instrument

concerto: music for a featured solo instrument (or instruments) and orchestra

condenser microphone: these produce a high-quality recording for audio; they need a power source such as a battery, and often contain two microphones or diaphragms to enable recordings in a variety of patterns

conjunct: melodic movement by step

consonant: sounds which fit well together (though the range of these chords or combinations of sound is not fixed)

continuo: this refers to the type of bass part written in the baroque period, consisting of a bass line with, sometimes, the addition of figures indicating the harmonies to be played – a figured bass. Normally played/realised by a keyboard instrument such as the harpsichord (whose player adds the harmonies) and a bass instrument

contrapuntal/polyphonic: a type of musical texture where different parts sing and/or play different notes using different rhythms

cresc. (crescendo): getting gradually louder

crotchet or quarter note: a common note-value, often (though not always) equivalent to one beat

cyclic: a composition where the theme recurs, possibly in different styles, throughout the work

D

da capo aria: an aria (solo song) in ternary form; it was normal practice for the singer to decorate the first section during its repetition

diatonic: music written using the major or minor keys; a major or minor scale, or the notes from such a scale

dim. (diminuendo): getting gradually quieter

diminished: usually refers to intervals such as fourth, fifth and seventh: these are one semitone less than a perfect fourth, perfect fifth or minor seventh respectively

diminution: (i) shortening the note values of a melody, usually by halving them; (ii) reducing the intervals within a melody (e.g. from movement by tone to movement by semitone)

disjunct: refers to melodic movement by leap

dissonant: sounds which clash when played together

dotted notes: a dot placed after a note adds half the original value of the note: so a dotted minim is worth three crotchets, a dotted crotchet is worth 1½ crotchets, and so on

double-stopping: the playing of two adjacent strings simultaneously (e.g. on violin, viola, cello, double bass)

drone: sustained note, or notes at a fixed pitch (as on bagpipes)

drum fill: usually heard at the end of a phrase, this is where the drummer plays a free rhythmic pattern to fill in the bars indicated

dynamic microphone: microphones which are relatively inexpensive but which tend to focus on a particular part of the frequency range

E

eighth note or quaver: a note lasting half a crotchet

equalisation (EQ): a function on multi-track recorders that allows you to adjust the relative balance of the frequencies present in your recording. Even the most basic multi-track recorder will have a mixing desk with three sections – low (bass), mid and high (treble). With these you can reduce or boost frequencies above or below a particular point (typically, bass below 100Hz, treble above 10 Hz, with mid EQ controlling the ranges in between these outer limits)

F

f (forte): loud

ff (fortissimo): very loud

falsetto: literally a 'false voice': singing by an adult male in a vocal register higher than that normally used. It is commonly used by male altos and countertenors as their regular mode of singing and also features in pop music

first movement form (more usually known as sonata form): consisting of three main sections: exposition, where the main themes or subjects are first heard; development, where ideas from the exposition are developed, passing through different keys; recapitulation, where the main themes return. Optional additional sections are the coda or codetta: rounding-off sections

flat: the lowering of pitch by a semitone; the name given to the black note to the left of a white note. Flats in key signatures are added in this order: B E A D G C F (the reverse order of sharps)

forte: loud

fortissimo: very loud

free rhythm: where the rhythm of the music is not set by regular bar lines but determined by the performer in response to the flow of the music

full close: alternative name for final cadences, i.e. perfect cadence (dominant to tonic chords) and plagal cadence (subdominant to tonic chords)

G

glissando/portamento/slide: sliding from one note to another

ground bass: music where a bass pattern (or melody in the bass) is repeated a number of times while the parts above alter

H

hairpins: term used to refer to the signs which can replace *crescendo* and *diminuendo*

half close or imperfect cadence: tonic, or another chord, to dominant; an incomplete cadence

half note or minim: a note lasting two crotchets

harmonic/homophonic: a type of musical texture where different parts sing and/or play different notes but move together in the same rhythm

hemiola: where two bars of 3/4 are played as three bars of 2/4 or one bar of 3/2 as in this example:

holistic: where the level of demand of the music performed will be assessed by taking into account the additional complication of performing on two instruments simultaneously (for example voice and guitar, or voice and piano)

homophonic/harmonic: a type of musical texture where different parts sing and/or play different notes but move together in the same rhythm

I

imitation: where entries copy (exactly or at least recognisably) the musical phrase which has just been heard

imperfect cadence (or half close): tonic, or another chord, to dominant; an incomplete cadence

improvisation: to make up or extemporise; in practice, improvisation is generally done 'on' a particular musical feature such as a melody, chord sequence or scale

interrupted cadence: dominant to (usually) submediant rather than the expected tonic

interval: the distance in pitch between two notes; you will be expected to understand intervals within the octave: these are major and minor seconds, thirds, sixths and sevenths; diminished, perfect and augmented fourths and fifths; diminished sevenths

inversion: turning a melody 'upside down' but keeping its intervals:

irregular rhythms: music where the time signature changes (usually a lot), or where the accents frequently shift

K

key: the tonal centre of the music, indicated by the presence of one or more sharps or flats (if there are no sharps or flats, the music is in C major or A minor)

key signature: sharp(s) or flat(s) placed at the beginning of the music and at the beginning of each subsequent line, to indicate the scale used and, therefore, the key of the music

L

layered: music built up of several strands; a term often applied to minimalist music, or the method of producing music in a recording studio

M

major: music based on a major scale, where the tones (T) and semitones (S) come in this order: TTSTTTS as in this example:

metre: refers to the use of a time signature; the number of beats in each bar

mf (mezzo forte): fairly loud

middle eight: term given to the contrasting section in a pop song, usually (but not necessarily) eight bars long

MIDI: Musical Instrument Digital Interface: the means by which messages about what is played, in terms of data regarding pitch, duration, intensity, tempo and so on, are transmitted

minim or half note: a note lasting two crotchets

minor: music based on a minor scale, where the tones and semitones in a melodic minor scale are, going up the scale, TSTTTTS and, coming down the scale, TTSTTST as in this example:

You might also have heard the minor scale in what is called its harmonic form:

minuet and trio: a dance style written in 3/4 time. The two sections are both in binary form, with the trio forming a contrast in style and/or orchestration with the minuet. Normally the minuet is played repeating each section, then the trio is played in the same way, and finally the minuet is played again without repeats

modal: (i) music which uses an early form of scale;

the most characteristic feature is usually a tone between the seventh and eighth notes of the scale. (ii) used within this specification as being different from major or minor; usually characterised by the use of the flattened seventh note of the scale (e.g. playing from D to another D on the keyboard, using only white notes); often a characteristic of folk music and some styles of popular music:

modulation: moving from one key to another

mordent: the insertion of the note above (upper mordent) or below (lower mordent) the written note

mp (mezzo piano): fairly quiet

muted (con sordino): placing a piece of wood against the bridge of a string instrument or altering the sound of a brass instrument by inserting a cone-shape into or covering the bell of the instrument

N

note values: the different note shapes represent different time-values. The main note names and their relative values are:

Semibreve	Whole Note	= 4 crotchets
Minim	Half Note	= 2 crotchets
Crotchet	Quarter Note	
Quaver	Eighth Note	= ½ a crotchet
Semiquaver	Sixteenth Note	= ¼ a crotchet

These notes look like:

A dot placed after a note adds half the original value of the note, so for instance a dotted minim is worth 3 crotchets, and so on.

O

octaves: playing or singing the same tune together at different octaves (see also unison)

ornamentation: decorating the written pitch

ostinato: a repeated musical phrase or rhythm

P

p (piano): quiet

pp (pianissimo): very quiet

passing note: a melodic note placed between two harmony notes which results in stepwise movement:

pentatonic: a scale based on five notes, such as C D F G A; the black notes of the piano produce such a scale

phrasing: dividing a melody into phrases or short units, e.g. question and answer

pianissimo (pp): very quiet

piano (p): quiet

pitch bend: technique associated with guitar playing: the player frets a string and then pushes it sideways to raise the pitch

pizzicato (of stringed instruments): plucking the strings instead of using a bow

polyphonic/contrapuntal: a type of musical texture where different parts sing and/or play different notes using different rhythms

polyrhythm: where several different rhythms are played or sung together

portamento/slide/glissando: sliding from one note to another

primary chords: chords based on the first, fourth and fifth notes of the scale; thus, in C major, chords/triads built on C, F and G

Q

quarter note or crotchet: a common note-value, often (though not always) equivalent to one beat

quaver or eighth note: a note lasting half a crotchet

R

rapping: speaking rhythmically, using a pattern of rhyming phrases over a musical backing

real time: when you play music, for instance into a sequencer, and record the actual rhythms that you play

regular rhythm: music which keeps to a single time signature

Roman numerals: these can can be used, alongside chord symbols, to identify chords within a scale. The example below shows the first four chords in C major:

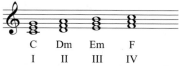

rondo form: music in at least five sections where the first section (A) is repeated after each new contrasting section (B, C, etc.), giving A B A C A

rubato: from the Italian for 'robbed': where the player uses a certain amount of freedom with the tempo to add expression to the music

S

scalic: melodic movement using a scale, moving upwards or downwards in steps

scherzo and trio: similar form to the minuet and trio, but faster, so that, although still in 3/4 time, there is just one beat per bar; the term scherzo is Italian for 'joke'

secondary chords: chords based on the second, third and sixth notes of the scale; in C major these are D minor, E minor and A minor

semibreve or whole note: a note lasting four crotchets

semiquaver or sixteenth note: a note lasting ¼ of a crotchet

semitone: the smallest difference in pitch used in most music; for example the distance from C to C or from E to F

sequence: the repetition of a phrase at a higher or lower pitch. A tonal sequence remains within the same key while a real sequence is in a new key:

sfz (sforzando): an accent; a note to be emphasised; also **sf**

sharp: raising the pitch of a note by a semitone; the name given to the black note to the right of a white note; sharps in key signatures are added in this order: F C G D A E B (the reverse order of flats)

simple time: time signatures where the beat is divided into two: typically, a crotchet beat divided into two quavers

single melody line: music with neither countermelody, descant nor other supporting lines

sixteenth note or semiquaver: a note lasting ¼ of a crotchet

slide/glissando/portamento: sliding from one note to another

sonata: a composition, usually in four movements, for one or two instruments

sonata form (also known as 'first movement form'): consisting of three main sections: exposition, where the main themes or subjects are first heard; development, where ideas from the exposition are developed, passing through different keys; recapitulation, where the main themes return. Optional additional sections are the coda or codetta: rounding-off sections

staccato: play the notes crisply and detached

step time: where you input the notes (for instance into a sequencer or computer program) one at a time, choosing the duration and pitch of each in turn

strophic: a song form in which the music is repeated (exactly or almost exactly) for each verse

T

tempo: the speed of the music

texture: refers to the number and type of sounds heard together; thus, a simple texture would consist of one or two lines of music; a more complex texture would occur when increasing numbers of different ideas are heard together (see harmonic, homophonic, contrapuntal, polyphonic)

theme and variations: a form in which an opening theme is subject to variations upon each successive repetition

through-composed: a song form in which the music changes continually to reflect the meaning of the words

tierce de Picardie: where the final chord of music in a minor key has a major third instead of the expected minor

timbre: the characteristic sounds of different instruments and voices; for this specification, it includes the use of technology, synthesised and computer-generated sounds, sampling, and the use of techniques such as reverb, distortion and chorus

tonal: having a tonal centre or a sense of key, belonging to a key

tone: the difference in pitch of two semitones, for instance from C to D

triadic: a type of melodic movement through the notes of a triad (e.g. C – E – G)

trill: the rapid alternation of two adjacent notes

trio: (i) a chamber group of three players; (ii) the middle section of a movement – minuet and trio, or scherzo and trio – in ternary form, and normally in 3/4 time. The trio usually forms a contrast in style and/or orchestration with the minuet or scherzo. The trio, like the minuet or scherzo that precedes it, is normally itself in binary form, with both sections repeated.

turn: a decoration of a written note, adding the pitches above and below

turntablism: turntables and a DJing mixer are used to create music by manipulating sounds. It involves moving the records on the turntables, moving the stylus and mixing the sounds. In this way, players perform using different turntable techniques including scratching, beat-matching and beat-mixing, combined via the mixer.

U

unison: playing or singing the same tune together, without harmony, at the same pitch (see also octaves)

vibrato: a rapid and regular fluctuation in pitch, used by instrumentalists and singers to produce a richer sound

VSTi: Virtual Studio instrument – a specific piece of software producing particular sets of sounds, some based on synthesised technology and others on sampling

W

whole note or semibreve: a note lasting four crotchets

whole tone scale: one which rises in whole tones:

with a bow (con arco): using a bow to produce a note on a string instrument

Index

A

a capella 53
accelerando 170
accents 14, 15
acciaccatura 27
appoggiatura 27
accompanists
performance as an accompanist 159
using 171
acoustic performances 152
annotation 174–175
assessment criteria 160–163
choosing 154
preparation 170–171
skills 158–159
added seventh 130
Africa, music of 80–83
alap 87
Alberti bass 132
annotation 115, 119, 120, 174–175
antiphonal music 25
appoggiatura 27
appraisal of compositions 91, 138–143
arch-shape form 38
Areas of Study (AoS) 7, 13
harmony and tonality 18–23, 98–99
rhythm and metre 14–17, 96–97
structure and form 36–41, 104–105
texture and melody 24–29, 100–101
timbre and dynamics 30–35, 102–103
arias 40, 53, 54
arpeggio 27
articulation 29
Assessment Objectives 8
augmentation 16

B

backbeats 70, 79
ballads 66
Baroque music 16, 46–49
bars 14, 96
barsuris 85
Beatles 68
beats 14, 15, 96
bhangra 87
bi-rhythm 17, 82
binary form 36, 48, 58, 104
blue notes 28, 63, 65
blues 62–63
bols 86
bpm 149
broken chords 24, 27

C

cadences 20, 51
cadenzas 50–51
call and response structure 37, 65, 80, 82
calypso 78
Candidate Record Form 149
canons 25, 52
cantatas 53
Caribbean, music of the 78–79
carnivals 78
chamber music 56–57
choirs 52
choral music
African 80
Western classical 52–53
chords 21, 22, 62, 130
broken 24, 27
power 69
chorus, electronic 32
chorus (refrain) 41, 66
choruses 53, 54, 73
chromatic music 18, 28
classical music 50
clave rhythm 79

click track 172
coda 130
composers
Baroque 47
Romantic 51
composition 90
appraisal of 91, 138–143
approaching 92–93
choosing 112, 130
examination preparation 146–147
final recording and presentation 148–149
further study 126–127
instrumental and vocal combinations 108–109
listening skills 122–123
musical elements 96–107, 124–125
notation 114–121
resources and 113, 131
using ICT 110–111
writing 132–135
compound time 14
compression 32, 167
computer software 110–111
con arco 33
con sordino 33, 170
concept albums 70
concertino 48
concerto grosse 48
concertos 48–49, 50–51
condenser microphones 164
conjunct melody 27
consonant harmony 18
context 74
continuo 47
contrapuntal texture 24, 46, 53, 80
contrasts 36
conventions 74, 91
crescendo 35
cross-rhythms 16
cycle 40, 82, 86

D

da capa aria 40, 41
dances, Baroque period 48
decrescendo 35
degrees of a scale 20, 26
development in sonata form 39
diatonic music 18, 28
diminuendo 35
diminution 16
disjunct melody 27
dissonance 18, 63, 98
distortion 32
DJs (disc jockeys) 72
dominant seventh chords 21
dotted notes 14
double-stopping 33
drones 19, 54, 84
drum fills 17
drum music
   African 82
   Caribbean 78
duets 59
Dylan, Bob 66
dynamic microphones 164
dynamics 34–35, 58, 103

E

ensembles 73, 159
episodes 38, 48, 50
EQ/equalisation 173
exposition in sonata form 39, 50

F

f (forte) 34
falsetto 33
feedback 69
ff (fortissimo) 34
fills 17, 41
film music 74–75
flats 23, 63
folk music 19, 54, 66
form and structure 36–41, 104–105
fp (forte-piano) 35
free rhythms 15
funk 72

fusion 64, 77
fz (forzata) 35

G

gat 87
genre 39
glissando 29, 170
gospel music 65
graphic notation 114, 117, 120
ground bass 41, 49
group performances 152, 159, 161, 171

H

'hairpins' 35
hard rock 71
harmonic texture 24, 80
harmonics 30, 47
harmony 18–21, 98
harpsichord 46, 58
hemiolas 16
hip-hop 72
holistic assessments 154
homophonic texture 24, 80
hooks 98

I

ICT and composition 110–111
idiomatic composition 90
imitation 25
imperfect cadence 20, 51
improvisation 29, 50, 74
India, music of 84–87
instruments
   African 83
   baroque period 46–47
   Caribbean 78
   chamber music 56–57
   Indian 84–85
   sonatas 58–59
   timbre 30–33, 102
   writing for 108
interrupted cadences 20
intervals 26
inversion 28

K

key signatures 23
keys 18, 23, 99
koras 83
kosikas 83

L

layered texture 25
legato 29
leitmotifs 74
lieder 55
listening skills 122–123
loops 72

M

madrigals 53
major scales 22, 23, 62
masses 52
matras 86
medieval music 19
melisma 55, 65
melody 26–29, 100–101
   African music 80
   Indian music 84, 85
   texture and 24, 25
mento 79
metre 14, 96
mf (mezzo forte) 34
microphones 164
middle 8 67, 104
MIDI 172
minor scales 22, 23
minuet and trio form 40, 48, 58
modes 23
modulation 23, 36, 99
molto 35
monophonic texture 25, 54
mordent 170
motet 53
mp (mezzo piano) 34
multi-track recording 32, 110, 173
musicals 73
mutes, playing with 33, 170

N

notation 114, 115
   annotation 115, 119
   choosing type to use 120–121
   graphic 114, 117
   staff 114, 116
   tab 115, 118

O

octaves 25
opera 54
oratorios 53
orchestra, Baroque period 46–47
ornamentation 29
ostinato 29
overtones 30
overtures 74

P

p (piano) 34
panning 32, 167
parallel motion 80
passing notes 27
pedal notes 19
pentatonic scales 28
perfect cadence 20
performances 152
   acoustic 152, 154, 158–163, 170–171
   annotation 174–175
   duration 153
   technology-based 153, 155, 164–167, 172–173
phrasing 29
pianos 58, 59
pitch bend 29, 118
pizzicato 57, 170
plagal cadence 20
poco a poco 35
polyphonic texture 24, 46, 53, 80
polyrhythm 17
popular music 61
   of 1960s 64–69
   African influence on 81
   blues 62–63
   film music 74–75

hip hop 72
   music theatre 73
   rock music 70–71
popular song forms 41, 67
portamento 29
power chords 69
pp (pianissimo) 34
primary chords 62, 130
progressive rock 70
psychedelic rock 70
pulse 14, 15
punk rock 71

R

rag 84, 86
ragas 87
rallentando 170
rapping 72, 154, 162
real time 110
recapitulation in sonata form 39
recitatives 53, 54
recordings, making the best 148–149
reggae 79
repetition 36, 62
requiem 52
reverberation 32
Renaissance music 16, 53
rhythm 14–17, 96–97
   African music 82
   blues 63
   Indian music 84, 86
rhythmic cycles 82
rhythm'n'blues 64
riffs 29, 79
ripieno 48
ritardando 170
ritenuto 170
rock music 70–71
rock steady 79
rock'n'roll 64
Rolling Stones 63, 68
Romantic music 51
rondo form 38, 48, 51, 104
rounds 25
rubato 17

S

sacred music 53
salsa 79
sam 86
samples 32, 72
sans rigueur 149
sarangis 84
scales 18
   degrees of a scale 20, 26
   intervals 26
   major and minor 22, 23, 62
   modes 23
   pentatonic 28
   whole tone 28
scalic melody 27
scherzo and trio form 40, 58
secondary chords 130
secular music 53
semitones 22, 23
sequence 28, 101
sequencers 32, 111, 172
sforzando 29, 35
sharps 23
shenhais 85
simple time 14
single line melody 25, 54
sitars 84
ska 79
slide 29
slur 29
Smith, Bessie 63
software 110–111
solo concerto 48, 50
solo performances 152, 154, 158, 171
solo sonatas 58
solo songs 54–55, 66, 73
sonata form 39, 50, 58, 105
sonatas 58–59
songs
   solo 54–55, 66, 73
   writing 105, 107
soul music 65
spirituals 65
staccato 29, 116
staff notation 114, 116, 120

steelbands 78
step time 110
Strands of Learning 7, 13, 42–43
   popular music 61–75
   Western classical tradition 46–59
   world music 77–87
strophic form 40, 54, 66, 105
structure and form 36–41, 104–105
suites 48
surprise cadences 20, 51
syncopation 16
synthesisers 32, 72

T

tab notation 115, 118, 120
tablas 84
tala 84, 86
technology-based performances 153
   annotation 174–175
   assessment criteria 155, 166–167
   preparation 172–173
   resources and requirements 155, 164–165
tempo 17
ternary form 37, 41, 104, 123
texture 24–25, 100
theme and variation form 38
through-composed form 40, 55, 105
tierce de Picardie 20, 49

timbre 30–33, 102
time signatures 14, 15, 96
tintal 86
tonal languages 80
tonality 22–23, 99
tones 22, 28
tonic chords 22
tremolo/temolando 33
très calme et doucement 149
triadic melody 27
triads 21
trills 29, 51, 170
trumpets 47
turn 29, 170
turntablism 154, 163
tutti 48, 50
12-bar blues 62

U

unison 25, 80

V

verse and chorus form 41, 66, 105
vibrato 33, 63
virtuoso performances 29, 70
vocoders 32
voices
   classical music for 52–55
   vocal techniques 33
   writing for 109
VSTi 172

W

Western Classical Tradition 46
   Baroque orchestral music 46–49
   chamber music 56–57
   the concerto 50–51
   music for voices 52–55
   the sonata 58–59
Who 69
whole tone scales 28
world music 77
   Africa 80–83
   Caribbean 78–79
   India 84–87

X

xylophones 83